The Geopolitics of TTIP

Repositioning the Transatlantic Relationship for a Changing World

Daniel S. Hamilton

Editor

Center for Transatlantic Relations
Paul H. Nitze School of Advanced International Studies
Johns Hopkins University

Hamilton, Daniel S., ed., *The Geopolitics of TTIP: Repositioning the Transatlantic Relationship for a Changing World*

Washington, DC: Center for Transatlantic Relations, 2014.

© Center for Transatlantic Relations, 2014

Center for Transatlantic Relations
The Paul H. Nitze School of Advanced International Studies
The Johns Hopkins University
1717 Massachusetts Ave., NW, Suite 525
Washington, DC 20036
Tel: (202) 663-5880
Fax: (202) 663-5879
Email: transatlantic@jhu.edu
http://transatlantic.sais-jhu.edu

ISBN 13: 978-0-9890294-9-0

Cover background image: Konstantin Sutyagin

Contents

Preface and Acknowledgments

The Transatlantic Trade and Investment Partnership (TTIP) being negotiated by the United States and the European Union is far more than just another trade agreement. Its economic impact is likely to be considerable for both sides of the North Atlantic, as well as for many others around the world. But TTIP's geostrategic implications may be equally profound, and are also likely to shape the final nature of an agreement. This book examines that dimension.

Our authors explore a range of geostrategic considerations with regard to TTIP. Their conclusions were informed by a series of meetings we have held on both sides of the Atlantic with government officials, TTIP negotiators, legislators, and a range of stakeholders engaged in TTIP debates. We have profited from the insights gathered from those discussions and thank our interlocutors for their participation. The views expressed in this volume, however, are those of the authors alone.

We conclude that while a successful TTIP would offer considerable geostrategic advantages to the United States and the European Union, it also presents some challenges. In addition, closer examination of TTIP's geopolitics reveals a number of next-order issues that governments still need to address. We offer recommendations in each of these areas.

This study is part of a broad-based effort by the Center for Transatlantic Relations, via our Transatlantic Partnership Forum and regular policy briefs, to explore TTIP's impact on key stakeholders and on the transatlantic relationship. It also complements our other writings in which we use both geographic and sectoral lenses to examine the deep integration of the transatlantic economy, and the role of the U.S. and Europe in the global economy, with particular focus on how globalization is affecting American and European consumers, workers, companies, and governments.

I would like to thank Miriam Cunningham for her tremendous assistance, as well as the Belgian and Finnish Ministries of Foreign Affairs; the European Union; the German Foreign Office; and the Transatlantic Program of the German government, with funds from the European

Recovery Program of the German Ministry for Economics and Technology, for their support. All authors write in their personal capacity, however, and none of the views expressed here represent those of any government or institution.

DANIEL S. HAMILTON
Executive Director
Center for Transatlantic Relations
School of Advanced International Studies
Johns Hopkins University

TTIP's Geostrategic Implications

Daniel S. Hamilton

The Transatlantic Trade and Investment Partnership (TTIP) currently under negotiation by the United States and the European Union (EU) promises to unleash significant opportunities to generate jobs, trade and investment across the Atlantic. While much analysis has been conducted regarding TTIP's potential economic impact, there has been relatively little exploration of its geostrategic implications.

TTIP at its core is an economic negotiation that in the end will stand or fall on its economic merits. Yet TTIP also reflects a broad new transatlantic consensus that the world that created the original transatlantic alliance is fading fast, and that Americans and Europeans must work more urgently to build a partnership that is more effective in generating economic opportunity and confidence at home; engaging other powers; and strengthening and extending basic norms and principles guiding the international system. These wider aims, in turn, are likely to influence TTIP's ultimate nature and content. Moreover, geopolitical considerations, not just economic calculus, are factors likely to strengthen or weaken support for TTIP among key constituencies both inside and outside the transatlantic community.

A successful TTIP would offer considerable geostrategic advantages to the United States and the European Union. Yet it also faces significant challenges. In addition, closer examination of TTIP's geopolitics reveals a number of next-order issues that governments still need to address. This chapter looks at each of these dimensions in turn.

Why TTIP? Why Now?

TTIP is not a new idea. Discussions of an ambitious transatlantic deal stretch back over two decades. A serious U.S.-EU negotiation was never launched, however, due to two lines of criticism. The first was that such a deal would be "too big," swamping the multilateral system and encompassing so many issues and reaching so deeply into American and European societies that it would invite opposition by too many interest groups.[1] Others argued that such a deal would be "too small," since transatlantic tariffs and other trade barriers were not that consequential.

Each of these arguments has faded. First, even though U.S. and European governments would prefer a global agreement on more open trade, the Doha Round of multilateral trade negotiations is stuck. The multilateral system administered by the WTO is under challenge, especially by a number of rapidly developing countries that show little interest in new market-opening initiatives and do not share the core principles or basic structures that underpin open rules-based commerce. As a result, the global economy is drifting dangerously towards the use of national discriminatory trade, regulatory and investment practices.

Second, even though transatlantic tariffs may be low, the transatlantic economy is so big that even small tariff reductions can be more important than big tariff cuts in smaller high-growth markets. Moreover, reducing or eliminating tariffs makes it easier to tackle regulatory differences, where even more substantial transatlantic economic gains could be made.

Third, the American and European economies are still struggling to recover from the Great Recession; TTIP offers an opportunity to generate jobs and growth without piling on additional government debt.

Fourth, TTIP is indeed a big negotiation. But the reality of deep integration between the U.S. and EU economies means that greater alignment and coherence on issues ranging from services and investment to regulatory differences could do far more to generate jobs and economic growth than a narrow focus on traditional trade barriers alone.

Finally, while there are regulatory and other differences between the United States and the European Union, on balance such differences pale in comparison with differences each has with many other countries. The addition of four billion people to the globalized economy and the rise of other powers, together with recent Western economic turmoil, have convinced U.S. and European decision-makers

---

[1] See the chapter by Charles Ries in this volume.

that the window of opportunity may be closing on the ability of Western countries to maintain high labor, consumer, health, safety and environmental standards and to advance key norms of the liberal rules-based order unless the United States and the European Union act more effectively together.

The Economic Dimension

The transatlantic economy generates $5 trillion in total commercial sales a year and employs up to 15 million workers. It is the largest and wealthiest market in the world, accounting for three-quarters of global financial markets and over half of world trade. It accounts for over 50% of world GDP in terms of value and 40% in terms of purchasing power. No other commercial artery is as integrated. Nonetheless, much more can be done to lower tariff and non-tariff barriers, spur services and investment and tackle unnecessary and costly regulatory differences.[2]

TTIP is first and foremost an economic negotiation seeking agreement in three pillars. The first pillar addresses such market access issues as tariffs and rules of origin. The second seeks to reduce, where feasible, non-tariff barriers and to find coherence, convergence or recognition of substantial equivalence between U.S. and EU approaches to specific regulatory issues. The third pillar seeks common agreement on a range of norms and standards regarding such issues as investment, intellectual property rights, discriminatory industrial policies and state-owned enterprises. Some of these standards are likely to extend prevailing WTO standards (WTO-plus); others could go beyond existing multilateral norms (WTO-extra).[3]

In addition, the TTIP will not necessarily be concluded with a final document; negotiators seek a "living agreement" that is likely to consist of new consultative mechanisms regarding regulatory and non-tariff issues that can anticipate or respond to evolving innovation, eco-

---

[2]For more on jobs, trade and investment between both sides of the North Atlantic, see Daniel S. Hamilton and Joseph P. Quinlan, *The Transatlantic Economy 2014: Annual Survey of Jobs, Trade and Investment between the United States and Europe* (Washington, DC: Center for Transatlantic Relations, 2014).

[3]See the chapter by Vera Thorstensen in this volume.

nomic friction due to changing legislation, or other developments in trade and technology.

Taken together, these elements underscore that TTIP is not just another trade agreement, it is a new-generation negotiation aimed at repositioning the U.S. and European economies for a more diffuse world of intensified global competition.

TTIP's economic impact depends upon the final nature of any arrangement. But if TTIP eliminates or reduces most transatlantic tariffs; lowers barriers to the services economy; aligns or reduces inefficiencies in regulatory discrepancies; and ensures continued high standards in such areas as labor, consumer, safety and health and environment, it is likely to boost jobs and growth significantly on both sides of the Atlantic.

According to the European think tank ECIPE, a transatlantic zero-tariff agreement could boost U.S. and EU exports each by 17%—about five times more than under the U.S.-Korea free trade agreement.[4] Even greater gains would be realized through reductions in non-tariff barriers and aligning regulatory standards. Estimates indicate that 80% of the overall potential wealth gains resulting from TTIP will come from cutting costs imposed by bureaucracy and regulation, as well as from liberalizing trade in services and public procurement.[5] Eliminating barriers to services would have a substantial impact on jobs and growth, since most American and European jobs are in the services economy.

To the extent that TTIP can help generate jobs, spark growth and reinvigorate the U.S. and European economies, it also promises to generate renewed confidence among publics and elites and ameliorate some of the political dysfunction afflicting many Western societies. Revived economic growth could help to re-legitimize the EU in the eyes of European voters and restore the efficacy of democratic institutions in the United States. TTIP cannot do this alone, of course, but it

---

[4]F. Erixon and M. Bauer, "A Transatlantic Zero Agreement: Estimating the Gains from Transatlantic Free Trade in Goods." ECIPE Occasional Paper No. 4/2010 (Brussels: ECIPE, 2010).

[5]Joseph Francois, project leader, "Reducing Transatlantic Barriers to Trade and Investment. An Economic Assessment" (London: Centre for Economic Policy Research, 2013).

can be part of broader-based efforts to reinvigorate Western economies. An economic and political recovery advanced in part by TTIP—particularly if it is seen to boost the middle class and small and medium-sized companies—would also underscore to voters the benefits of openness and international engagement rather than protectionism and turning inward.[6] Greater confidence and economic vigor at home, in turn, has the potential to increase the magnetic pull of Western values elsewhere, underwrites U.S. and EU diplomatic capacity, and enhances possibilities for strategic outreach. Economic revival at home is an essential underpinning for continued transatlantic leadership in the wider world, because the normative appeal and continued relevance of the U.S. and European models for others depends heavily on how well they work for their own people.

TTIP's potential economic value ranges beyond the transatlantic market itself. Properly constructed, it can also be a useful policy initiative to help open global markets. TTIP reflects a growing recognition on both sides of the Atlantic that the United States and the EU must invest in new forms of transatlantic collaboration to strengthen multilateral rules and lift international standards. Given the size and scope of the transatlantic economy, standards negotiated by the United States and the EU can quickly become the benchmark for global models, reducing the likelihood that others will impose more stringent, protectionist requirements for either products or services, or that lower standards could erode key protections for workers, consumers or the environment.

Broader Geopolitical Advantages

TTIP, however, is about more than trade. It is about creating a more strategic, dynamic and holistic U.S.-EU relationship that is more confident, more effective at engaging third countries and addressing regional and global challenges, and better able to strengthen the ground rules of the international order. Let us look at each of these elements in turn.

---

[6]See the chapter by Charles Kupchan in this volume.

TTIP and the Transatlantic Community

TTIP is politically important to the U.S-EU relationship itself. TTIP is rooted in a core truth: despite the rise of other powers the United States and Europe remain the fulcrum of the world economy, each other's most important and profitable market and source of onshored jobs, each other's most important strategic partner, each other's closest partner in terms of values, and still a potent force in the multilateral system—when the two partners work in concert. The U.S.-EU relationship remains a foundational element of the global economy and the essential underpinning of a strong rules-based international order. Americans and Europeans literally cannot afford to neglect it. TTIP is evidence that the two partners are committed to open transatlantic markets, strengthen global rules and leverage global growth.

Despite this strength and potential, the U.S.-EU relationship regularly punches below its weight and fails to capitalize on significant opportunities for American and European citizens, companies, workers, consumers and the multilateral system they helped bring to life. In recent years the relationship has being buffeted by daunting economic challenges on each side of the Atlantic. Without U.S. fiscal solvency, economic growth, job creation and an end to partisan gridlock, Washington is unlikely to be the type of consistent, outward-looking partner that Europeans need and want. The United States has the same stake in Europe's success. Europe's protracted sovereign debt crisis and anemic economic recovery threaten to drain U.S. confidence in Europe and its institutions and derail American support for major transatlantic policy initiatives. The single most important effort the partners could make to improve their ability to act together abroad is for each to get its act together at home. To the extent that TTIP can energize growth and restore mutual confidence, it can help get the relationship back on track.

TTIP would break new ground in a number of ways. It would be the first congressionally-ratified agreement between the United States and the European Union. It would be the first real channel enabling the United States and the EU to forge a global partnership more relevant to 21st century challenges and opportunities. TTIP's "living agreement" provisions would constitute a pioneering effort to address the interrelationship between regulatory standards and open markets in a global economy. U.S.-EU agreement on basic norms and standards regarding issues ranging from state-owned enterprises and intellectual property to investment and consumer safety, and to act together to uphold such standards around the world, would be a first.

In this sense TTIP can also be an operational reflection of basic values shared across the Atlantic. TTIP's fundaments are those of democratic societies rooted in respect for human rights and the rule of law. The United States and the European Union are among the few entities that include basic labor, environmental and consumer protections in their trade agreements. They boast the two most sophisticated regulatory systems in the world. An agreement that commits both parties to sustain and uphold such principles and protections, not only vis-a-vis each other but together around the world, would be a strong affirmation of common values and a powerful instrument to ensure that such standards advance globally.

In all these ways, TTIP can be both a symbolic and practical assertion of Western renewal, vigor and commitment, not only to each other but to high rules-based standards and core principles of international order. It can be assertive, yet need not be aggressive. It challenges fashionable notions about a "weakened West."

TTIP can also serve to reassure each side of the Atlantic about each other. In recent years the transatlantic relationship has been challenged less because either partner assigns lesser value to the same norms, but rather that both have assigned lesser value to each other, due in particular to the shift away from Europe as the central theater of world affairs to a more diffuse world, which is exacerbated by the mix of generational and ethnic change within American politics towards cohorts who put less value on relations with Europe. The challenge is less that of rising antipathy than a degree of apathy, not more conflict but rather less priority.[7]

This relative inattention had had political consequences. In many quarters NATO is perceived to be wobbly. Moreover, a military alliance is insufficient as the sole anchor to what is a much broader and deeper transatlantic community of values and interests. Many

---

[7]See Bruce W. Jentleson, "Normative Future: A U.S. Perspective," in Daniel Hamilton and Kurt Volker, eds., *Transatlantic 2020: A Tale of Four Futures* (Washington, DC: Center for Transatlantic Relations, 2012).

Europeans are worried that the U.S. "pivot" to Asia will translate into less U.S. attention and commitment to Europe. Creation of what would essentially be a Euro-American market, together with a commitment to work together to advance core Western norms and standards, would offer reassurance that Europe is in fact America's "partner of choice" and that the pivot to Asia is not a pivot away from Europe.[8] Europeans are more likely to have greater faith in America's security commitments if they are anchored by strong trade and investment links. TTIP would also be an important U.S. validation of EU legitimacy that many Europeans crave, while reassuring Americans that the European Union is committed to look outward rather than inward. It would provide a new sense of purpose and direction for the transatlantic relationship at a time when transatlantic solidarity has been challenged by Russia's forceful annexation of the Crimean region of Ukraine and its direct military intervention to support armed separatists in other parts of the country.

Some proponents have characterized TTIP as an "economic NATO." This is a mistake that easily invites misinterpretation. In the American political context, the term "economic NATO" can be convenient shorthand to convey that TTIP is about a renewed sense of transatlantic solidarity. But for many Europeans the term doesn't translate so readily. The term's military allusion, for instance, conveys the impression that TTIP is directed against a particular threat, which it is not. In addition, NATO is dominated by one large military superpower, whereas TTIP is comprised of two roughly equal economic entities; references to an "economic NATO" offer unnecessary fodder to European critics concerned that the TTIP is a thinly veiled U.S. effort to assert economic dominance and steamroll the European way of life. And for other Europeans who are worried about America's staying power in Europe, the term raises concern that the United States may be diluting its strategic commitment to Europe in favor of a more transactional commercial partnership. For all of these reasons, TTIP is best characterized as offering a second anchor to the transatlantic partnership, in addition to NATO, and not as an "economic NATO."

---

[8]For suggestions on how Europe and the United States together should pivot to Asia, see Hans Binnendijk, ed., *A Transatlantic Pivot to Asia* (Washington, DC: Center for Transatlantic Relations, 2014).

TTIP is also important to each partner's own goals for itself. The United States, for example, is also negotiating a second mega-regional economic agreement, the Trans-Pacific Partnership, with 11 other Asia-Pacific partners. If TTIP and TPP are successful, the United States and its partners will have opened trade and investment across both the Atlantic and the Pacific with countries accounting for two-thirds of global output. Since the United States is the only party to both initiatives, the negotiations give Washington a distinct advantage in leveraging issues in one forum to advance its interests in the other, while potentially reinvigorating U.S. global leadership. The European Union is also negotiating a series of additional trade agreements with Asian and other partners, and TTIP offers the EU additional leverage in its negotiations with third countries. TTIP is also important to generate growth and jobs within Europe, to win greater popular support for the EU, particularly in countries like the United Kingdom, and to spur implementation of some of the EU's own goals, such as completion of the Single Market.

Terms of Engagement: Working with Other Powers

A quarter of a century ago, the opening of the Iron Curtain and the end of the Cold War reinforced the notion that Western liberal democracy was on the march. Those assumptions have been challenged in recent years, however, by Western economic and political turmoil; the rise of alternative models of state capitalism; Moscow's confrontational tactics; reluctance by emerging powers that are also democracies, such as Brazil and India, to fully associate themselves with the West or to consider themselves stakeholders for the international rules-based order; and the tumult and violence that followed the initial promise of the Arab Awakening.[9] What had been a sense of global convergence around such Western norms as rule-based institutions of collaboration, open non-discriminatory trading rules, the "democratic peace," and the "Washington consensus" on development has given way to a broader and more complex global competition of ideas over such issues as multilateralism, the use of force, the rights and responsibilities of state sovereignty, international justice, and

---

[9]See, for example, G. John Ikenberry, *Liberal Leviathan: The Origins, Crisis, and Transformation of the American World Order* (Princeton: Princeton University Press, 2011)

alternative models for domestic governance, particularly the relationship between state and market.[10]

In this sense, TTIP is important in terms of how the transatlantic partners together might best relate to rising powers, especially the emerging growth markets. Whether those powers choose to challenge the current international order and its rules or promote themselves within it depends significantly on how the United States and Europe engage, not only with them *but also with each other*.[11] The stronger the bonds among core democratic market economies, the better their chances of being able to include rising partners as responsible stakeholders in the international system. The more united, integrated, interconnected and dynamic the international liberal order—shaped in large part by the United States and Europe—the greater the likelihood that emerging powers will rise within this order and adhere to its rules. The looser or weaker those bonds are, the greater the likelihood that rising powers will challenge this order. So a key element of strategy in a G20/WTO world must be to protect and reinforce the institutional foundations of the liberal order, beginning with the partnership between the United States and Europe. This means not only refraining from imposing such national protectionist measures as trade tariffs, export subsidies or buy national policies, but coordinating efforts to ensure high standards globally that can both lift the lives of Americans and European and create economic opportunity for billions of others around the globe.

There are already signs that TTIP is affecting third countries. TTIP was "the elephant in the room" at the 2013 EU-Brazil summit; it is causing Brazilian leaders to reframe how they think of their evolving role and position.[12] Japan's decision to join the TPP arguably was due as much to the start of TTIP negotiations as to inner-Asian dynamics. With the EU now also negotiating a bilateral trade agreement with Japan, both the United States and the EU are in direct talks

---

[10]Jentleson, *op. cit.*

[11]See the contributions by Robert Hormats and Kemal Kirişci in this volume. Also Stuart E. Eizenstat, "Transatlantic Trade and Investment Partnership (TTIP) Remarks," Woodrow Wilson International Center for Scholars, (Washington, DC: March 21, 2013), http://www.acus.org/files/transcripts/seizenstat130321wilsonremarks.pdf.

[12]See the chapter by Vera Thorstensen and Lucas Ferraz in this volume.

with Tokyo about opening the Japanese market—a goal that for decades has seemed unattainable. There is also some reason to believe that the trade facilitation deal struck by WTO members in Bali in December 2013 was due in part to concern by various holdout countries that with the TTIP and TPP the global trading system was moving ahead without them.

TTIP has particular meaning for U.S. and EU relations with China and with Russia.

TTIP is lazily portrayed as an effort to confront and isolate China. Yet is less about containing China than about the terms and principles guiding China's integration and participation in the global economy. China's burgeoning trade with both the United States and Europe attests to U.S. and EU interest in engaging China, not isolating it. Yet Beijing has yet to embrace some basic tenets of the international rules-based order, and has sought to translate its economic clout into military influence, for instance saber-rattling on territorial claims in the South China Sea; or into diplomatic and political influence, for instance by holding down the value of its currency to boost its companies, leveraging its near-monopoly on rare earths to advance its strategic objectives, or directing state-owned companies not just to generate profits but to wield power on its behalf. TTIP, TPP and related initiatives are important instruments to help frame Beijing's choices—by underscoring China's own interests in an open, stable international system as well as the types of norms and standards necessary for such a system to be sustained. China itself has changed its position and signaled a willingness to join plurilateral talks on services. Its motivations remain unclear, but there is no denying that TTIP and related initiatives are injecting new movement and energy into efforts to open markets and strengthen global rules.

One anecdote may illustrate the point that joint or complementary U.S. and EU efforts may succeed where individual efforts have failed. Some years ago American and European publics were concerned that toys with unacceptably high lead content—including the iconic Barbie doll—were being imported from China. Washington told Beijing that American consumers still wanted relatively inexpensive toys from China, but that toys with such levels of lead simply did not meet the U.S. standard. The Americans had little success. Separately, EU officials told their Chinese counterparts that Brussels wanted to keep trade flowing, but that toys with high lead levels simply did not meet EU standards. They were also rebuffed. Rather than launch a trade war, U.S. and EU officials had a common conversation with the Chinese about the need to keep trade open while raising consumer standards, especially with regard to health and safety. The result was a trilateral U.S.-EU-China review process of consumer product safety, including biennial "summits" among relevant officials, which has had some modest success in gaining Chinese commitments to cooperate in applying product safety controls along supply and distribution chains; promoting company management systems that incorporate safety into product design; exchanging information regularly on major safety issues; reinforcing consumer product traceability; implementing the concept of seamless surveillance;[13] and exploring jointly the possible convergence of consumer product safety requirements.[14] Expansion of such cooperation in additional areas and with additional countries, based on alignment of U.S. and EU understandings regarding high levels of protection, promises to keep standards high while keeping markets open.

TTIP is also important with regard to U.S. and EU relations with Russia and Eurasia. TTIP is a values-based, rules-based initiative that is likely to strengthen Western economic and social cohesion, reinforce U.S. commitment to Europe, strengthen transatlantic energy ties, and contribute to greater attractiveness of the Western model. TTIP would also bolster the resilience of central and east European economies, stimulate U.S. investment and enable such countries to more easily resist Russian encroachment. These changes are likely to resonate across Wider Europe, especially Ukraine, Moldova, Georgia and even Belarus.

---

[13]Seamless surveillance links product safety controls along the product supply chain by enhancing cooperation between product safety authorities in countries of origin and countries where the products are sold.

[14]See, for example, the Press Statement of the Fourth Biennial Consumer Product Safety Trilateral Summit, 19 June 2014, available at http://ec.europa.eu/consumers/safety/international_cooperation/trilateral_cooperation/docs/20140617_press_statement_en.pdf; "Mattel Recalls Millions of Toys in Europe," Deutsche Welle, August 14, 2007, http://www.dw.de/mattel-recalls-millions-of-toys-in-europe/a-2738985.

This is anathema to the current leadership in the Kremlin. TTIP presents a huge challenge to the Kremlin's efforts to divide Europeans from Americans. It offers something that the Kremlin cannot match: a transparent, mutually beneficial agreement that creates a rules-based framework for international cooperation. A reinvigorated transatlantic marketplace among highly-connected, highly-competitive democracies, whose people enjoy greater economic growth and rising standards of living, would challenge the Kremlin's version of "managed democracy;" render Russia's own one-dimensional natural-resource-based economic model increasingly unattractive; and consign its rival economic project, the Eurasian Economic Union, to irrelevance.[15] Greater U.S.-EU energy cooperation would blunt Russia's monopolistic approach to European energy markets. And if such benefits extended to non-EU neighbors, particularly Ukraine, Russians themselves are likely to ask why their own country can't be better run.

For all these reasons, the Kremlin is conducting "active measures" in eastern Europe, and in the EU itself, including tactics of pressure and intimidation, to derail the TTIP. The West should push back while indicating a readiness to engage with Russia economically on the basis of the very rules and procedures being advanced through the TTIP. The message is not that the West is excluding Russia, but that Russia is excluding itself from this promising dynamic.

TTIP and the International Rules-Based Order

For more than two centuries, either Europeans or Americans, or both together, have been accustomed to setting global rules. In the post-World War II era the United States and the evolving European Union, each in its own way, has been a steward of the international rules-based order. Yet as new powers rise, older powers rise again, and the West faces challenges at home, the prospect now looms that Europeans and Americans could become standard-takers rather than standard-makers.[16]

---

[15]See the chapter by Edward Lucas in this volume.

[16]See Daniel S. Hamilton, "Transatlantic Challenges: Ukraine, TTIP and the Struggle to be Strategic," in Nathaniel Copsey and Tim Haughton, eds., *Journal of Common Market Studies Annual Review of the European Union in 2013*, September 2014.

Europeans and Americans share an interest in extending prosperity through multilateral trade liberalization. The December 2013 Bali agreement on trade facilitation is a sign that piecemeal progress can be made. But the overall Doha Round has been underway for almost a decade and a half with no agreement in sight, and the WTO system is under challenge, especially from emerging growth markets that have benefited substantially from the system.

Given this situation, EU and U.S. officials are using TTIP to unblock the WTO Doha negotiations and jumpstart multilateral negotiations. There is precedent for this. When the Uruguay Round stalled in the early 1990s, the United States, Canada and Mexico negotiated the North American Free Trade Agreement in just 14 months in 1992; it came into force in 1994. This plurilateral effort had a catalytic effect on the multilateral system; the Uruguay Round restarted and concluded successfully. The Information Technology Agreement negotiated by the United States and the EU also eventually became the basic multilateral agreement in this area. With the Doha Round stalled, we may again be at a point where plurilateral initiatives can ultimately reenergize the multilateral system.

Even a successful Doha Round agreement, however, would not address a host of issues that were not part of its mandate and yet are critical to the United States, the European Union, and the global economy. In this regard TTIP can be a pioneering effort to extend the multilateral system to new areas and new members. Each of TTIP's three pillars has the potential either to strengthen and expand multilateral rules (WTO-plus), or to generate standards and norms in new areas beyond the current system (WTO-extra).

TTIP's market access pillar, for instance, could potentially result in clearer, more straightforward and transparent rules of origin arrangements that could serve as the basis for future preferential rules of origin. Clear, simple and aligned rules of origin would facilitate global trade and thus serve as a common public good.[17]

---

[17]For more on the impact of TTIP on emerging powers and the international system, see Daniel S. Hamilton, "TTIP, implicaciones para las potencias emergentes y el orden internacional," *Puentes*, Volume 15, Number 6, 2014.

TTIP's second pillar could pioneer new ways for countries to ensure high standards for consumers, workers, companies and the environment while sustaining the benefits of an open global economy. New consultative mechanisms among regulatory agencies, including as part of TTIP's "living agreement" provisions, could eliminate redundant regulations, identify more efficient procedures, and avoid conflicts that create unnecessary costs for companies and consumers, while ensuring high standards that can prevail not only across the Atlantic but around the world. Mutual recognition of essentially equivalent norms and regulatory coherence across the transatlantic space not only promises economic benefits at home but could form the core of broader international norms and standards.

The standards being negotiated as part of TTIP's third pillar are intended to be more rigorous than comparable rules found in the WTO. Agreement on such issues as intellectual property, services, discriminatory industrial policies or state-owned enterprises could strengthen the normative underpinnings of the multilateral system by creating benchmarks for possible future multilateral liberalization under the WTO. U.S.-EU agreement on such principles, and agreement to act together to advance such norms globally, could not only take the international trading system further but establish broader political principles regarding the rule of law, human rights, labor, environmental and consumer standards.

Not only does TTIP have the potential to reinvigorate the multilateral system, it can also have positive knock-on effects in other regions. If a transatlantic free trade area does indeed help advance economic integration in other regions, the benefits promise to be geopolitical as well as economic in nature. As the United States and Europe become less able and willing to provide public goods, and as international institutions (such as the G-20 and the UN Security Council) become more unwieldy due to increases in membership, regional institutions may well have to pick up the slack. It could well be that bodies like ASEAN, the Gulf Cooperation Council, the African Union and the Pacific Alliance become ever more important contributors to governance and security in their respective regions. Developing the capacities of regional institutions is thus an important investment in future stability. To the degree that TTIP helps encourage integration and capacity building in other regions, it would have geopolitical benefits well beyond the Atlantic area. As Europe's own history has demonstrated, economic integration can usefully serve as the leading edge of political cooperation. A transatlantic pact that offers a benchmark for global standards can also spur other trade groupings to advance liberalization. Such "competitive regionalism" was a factor in the 1990s as trade groupings from Europe, South America, North America, and the Asia-Pacific all made significant steps forward. With global liberalization stalled for the foreseeable future, regional pacts may well again play a vanguard role. And TTIP has significant potential to get the ball rolling.

Since TTIP is not just about achieving greater regulatory coherence across the Atlantic, but about setting global benchmarks, it is more ambitious than the Trans-Pacific Partnership. In fact, a successful TTIP would actually be a TPP-plus agreement with regard to regulatory coherence and potentially with regard to WTO-plus and WTO-extra norms. In this sense, TTIP is likely to have more impact on Asian economies than TPP is likely to have on European economies.

Thinking much further ahead, the United States and the EU could also codify and align their respective free trade agreements to boost the multilateral system. An alignment and extension of free-trade arrangements among the United States, EU and all partners with whom they have such free-trade agreements would be a major boost to the global order.

For all these reasons, those who worry that TTIP could threaten the multilateral economic system should consider that the opposite may in fact be true. Although the notion of an ambitious transatlantic compact has been discussed since the early 1990s, the United States and the EU refrained from going ahead, partly out of concern for the multilateral system. Yet two decades later, the Doha Round has achieved little and the multilateral system faces erosion. TTIP has the potential to jump-start multilateralism, while serving as a laboratory for the WTO and vanguard for the rest of the world. The alternative is growing protectionism, U.S.-EU rivalry in third markets, and the triumph of lowest-common-denominator standards for health and safety. The absence of agreed rules and procedures across the Atlantic weakens the leverage of each region to ensure that high standards prevail elsewhere.

Challenges

Getting a TTIP deal will be tough. Remaining transatlantic tariff barriers, especially in agriculture, often reflect the most politically difficult cases. Long phase-in periods may be needed to eliminate tariff and quota barriers completely. Some of the most intense transatlantic disagreements have arisen over differences in regulatory policy. Issues such as food safety or environmental standards have strong public constituencies and are often extremely sensitive in the domestic political arena. Responsibility for regulation is split in the EU between Brussels and the member states, and in the United States between the federal and state governments. Investment barriers, especially in terms of infrastructure and transport sector ownership, will be very difficult to change. There is considerable debate how and whether to include financial services. It is questionable whether either side is prepared to gore its sacred cows on the TTIP altar—audiovisual for the EU, the Jones Act for the United States. Defense trade seems off limits.

The inclusion of regulatory elements into the TTIP has generated considerable confusion. Many critics believe that U.S. or EU regulations and laws are being tossed into the pot of inevitable trade-offs and deals associated with trade negotiations. They are concerned that EU negotiators, for instance, might concede to lower EU standards on genetically-modified organisms in order to open U.S. public procurement to European companies; or that U.S. negotiators might lower U.S. consumer protection laws to gain better access for American agricultural exports. Yet TTIP's regulatory dimension is not about creating thousands of unified transatlantic regulations. That would require re-legislating an uncountable series of domestic laws on each side of the Atlantic. That is neither feasible nor desirable, and is not the goal of the negotiation.

Both U.S. and EU officials have been clear that TTIP will not undermine existing levels of protection. It will reinforce each side's right to regulate, but now informed by common consultations and a process that can create greater trust and confidence in each other's regulatory processes and decisions. TTIP's regulatory pillar is about finding efficiencies, eliminating redundancies, or aligning regulatory processes to avoid conflicts that create unnecessary costs for companies and consumers, while ensuring high standards that can prevail not only across the Atlantic but around the world. The nature of such regulatory alignment is likely to vary depending on the particular sector involved. Accords might involve mutual recognition agreements; mutual recognition of the "substantial" or "essential" equivalence of each other's regulatory regimes and testing procedures; sharing of data regarding particular safety or health considerations; creating new consultative mechanisms among regulatory agencies; and other innovations. Yet this message has not really come through.

Investor-state dispute settlement mechanisms envisaged under TTIP could present the biggest challenge of all. Some view the issue as a self-imposed wound, offering little gain at great pain. Investment flows freely across the Atlantic; few potential investors are deterred due to fear of arbitrary, discriminatory court action or regulatory takings. Yet the issue could awaken an unholy alliance of sovereigntists and populists on both sides of the Atlantic. Others argue that the investor-state issue goes to the heart of TTIP's role as a regulatory pace-setter and that it is essential to a ground-breaking agreement.

Part of the problem is that TTIP's potential pains can be translated into negative, personalized anecdotes, TTIP's potential gains are more abstract and broad. U.S. and European officials need to do a better job offering positive examples of TTIP benefits that can resonate with average citizens.

These concerns and uncertainties underscore the importance of managing expectations while building a more energetic and effective outreach effort to both public and elite audiences. Such strategies should convey not only what TTIP is, but what it is not. It isn't a supranational regime. It will not contravene domestic laws. It isn't a threat to the American or European way of life. It is a means to generate jobs, open markets, and ensure high standards for the food we eat, the products we buy and the services we receive, in a world in which good jobs are being lost and those standards are under assault.

Political uncertainties also abound. Legislative approval could be difficult. TTIP is likely to be a "mixed agreement" for the EU, meaning that it will require approval not only by the European Parliament, but by 28 member state parliaments as well. On the U.S. side, USTR Michael Froman has committed negotiators to concluding an agreement on "a single tank of gas," meaning before the end of President

Obama's term in office in early 2017. But the Administration has not yet secured Trade Promotion Authority for either the TPP or TTIP. Without it, each agreement would be subject to potentially debilitating Congressional amendments. And the outcome of negotiations and a subsequent ratification debate would be even more uncertain if extended to a new President and Congress.

Seemingly unrelated or unanticipated third issues might also appear that could damage or even derail the negotiations, for instance a British referendum rejecting EU membership; war with Iran or conflagration in the Middle East; renewed economic crisis; an environmental disaster or terrorist attack, etc. The most prominent current issue is the disclosure of extensive spying operations by the U.S. National Security Agency against European allies and other governments, which has eroded mutual trust and confidence to such an extent that some in Europe are calling for the EU to suspend various agreements with the United States and to halt TTIP negotiations. Thus far European leaders have resisted such demands, as they know that TTIP is far more than just another trade agreement and that Europe has a great stake in a successful outcome to the negotiations. But the issue remains unresolved. The political reality is that if TTIP is ever to be ratified successfully, a U.S.-EU data protection package must be achieved in the same time frame as TTIP, especially since it is a "mixed agreement."

This list of difficult issues has raised concern that TTIP could divide rather than unite Europeans and Americans. Thus far both parties have signalled strong political commitment to a successful TTIP agreement. But as the going gets tough and other issues intrude, the open question remains whether both sides will consider that they need each other enough to make TTIP a priority and invest the political capital that will be needed to see the deal through to successful ratification and implementation.

Next-Order Questions

In addition to these challenges, governments have yet to address adequately a number of next-order issues that could draw out TTIP's full economic and geopolitical advantages.

Energy

TTIP has become important in the context of changing transatlantic energy realities. More effective energy cooperation originally was not a major impetus for the talks, but should now be incorporated to facilitate U.S. energy exports to Europe as part of a more strategic transatlantic approach to energy cooperation.[18]

Recent events in Ukraine and Russia have made clear that creating a transatlantic energy market is about more than economic efficiency. Energy cooperation has become an indispensable pillar of the Western community. Today the EU produces only a small portion of its energy needs, importing about 80% of its oil and about 60% of its gas. More than a third of this oil and 30% of the gas is of Russian origin. Some EU member states are 100% dependent on Russia for their gas needs.

Over the past few years America's oil and gas boom has rendered the United States over 80% self-sufficient in energy production and use. It will soon become an exporter of natural gas and surpass both Russia and Saudi Arabia to become the world's largest producer of oil and liquid natural gas.

A successful TTIP would enable the United States to export gas to Europe, since U.S. law prohibits such exports (or requires onerous licensing procedures) except to countries with which the United States has a free trade agreement. In essence, members of the TTIP and the Trans-Pacific Partnership alike should be eligible for waivers to Department of Energy licensing requirements. In addition, TTIP could enable the United States and the EU to align standards in areas such as e-mobility and energy efficiency, reduce tariff and non-tariff barriers to clean energy goods and services, and create mechanisms for mutual recognition of regulatory processes regarding energy innovation. It also offers a mechanism for the United States and the EU to agree on basic normative principles that could have important global repercussions. One example is mandatory access for third parties to pipelines in the hands of a monopoly. Both U.S. and EU law provide for this, but if extended more broadly as an international norm it

---

[18]The EU has proposed such an effort, see http://www.scribd.com/doc/233022558/EU-Energy-Non-paper.

would have significant impact on countries such as Ukraine or those in Central Asia.

Some critics are skeptical that substantial U.S. energy could flow to Europe anytime soon, given the fact that it will take years to build appropriate new infrastructure to send and receive American gas. They also note that LNG from the United States will never flow to Europe in large enough quantities to replace the 160 billion cubic meters the EU imports from Russia.

Such criticisms miss the point that even small amounts of LNG can be important bargaining tools for countries otherwise dependent on Russia as a monopoly supplier; just the prospect of American gas flows to Europe has forced Russia to break the link between oil and gas prices and to negotiate better terms with a number of European customers, including in Germany, Poland and Lithuania. And while it will take time to build new infrastructure, likely investors are deciding *today* on such multi-year projects. A strong U.S.-EU political signal of intent to build a more strategic energy partnership, including through TTIP, can influence such investment decisions, even as it sends a strong message of transatlantic solidarity in the face of Russian troublemaking.

The Issue of Openness

A second issue also requires greater definition and clarity. Despite TTIP's inherent potential to leverage U.S-EU efforts to engage rising powers on the terms of their integration into the international rules-based order, governments have not stated whether and how the eventual TTIP agreement, once concluded, might be open to others willing and able to commit to similar goals and ground rules. USTR Mike Froman has characterized TTIP as an "open platform," but the two parties have made no official statement to this effect. This stands in contrast to the TPP, where the United States and its negotiating partners have stated explicitly that the TPP is open to other APEC members (including China and Russia) and in principle much of the Asia-Pacific region.[19]

Framing the TTIP as an element of "open architecture" accessible to others could give the West tremendous leverage in terms of ensur-

---

[19]TPP Leaders Statement, Honolulu, Hawaii, 12 November 2011.

ing ever broader commitment to the high standards and basic principles governing modern open economies, much as NATO and EU enlargement gave the West significant leverage over transitional democracies in central and eastern Europe. Once reason why many Turks are interested in TTIP, for instance, is that it represents a "transatlantic form of governance" rooted in the rule of law, as opposed to authoritarian or dirigiste models, and thus is important as a means to influence Turkey's own modernization.[20]

The fact that the United States and the European Union have not yet stated that TTIP is part of an open architecture of trade, however, contributes to concern among other countries that TTIP is a "West against the rest" initiative, and thus more about trade diversion that trade creation. It invites counterbalancing coalitions and undermines TTIP's own rationale as a values-driven lever to open global markets.

As a first step, President Obama and EU leaders should issue a Leaders Statement that TTIP is part of an open architecture of trade. Such a Statement does not yet need to outline modalities. The Leaders Statement could also announce that the two parties are initiating consultative/information mechanisms for third parties potentially affected by a final agreement, recognizing that some of this is already underway.

Once such a Statement is made, further internal work should be done to make it operational. The underlying premise is that the TTIP package would be opened only after negotiated. On this basis, various options may be worth exploring. One is straightforward accession; countries that are willing and able to meet the same high standards as negotiated could accede. There may be an option to open individual elements to others, for instance market access or signing on to basic investment principles. This option would recognize that there are likely to be limits as to how open TTIP can be. For instance, it will be difficult simply to open some regulatory arrangements that might emerge from TTIP, or to open the "living agreement" aspect of a TTIP process, because such elements are likely to be based on trust and confidence generated among U.S. and EU regulators, legislators and certifiers. But countries may be able to join or attach themselves

---

[20]See Kemal Kirişci's chapter in this volume.

to some provisions. For instance, when the United States and EU finalized their Open Skies agreement on transatlantic air transport in 2007, legal texts were created enabling a range of additional countries, not only in Europe but in other parts of the world, to also implement provisions of the agreement through separate accords.[21]

Special arrangements might be needed for countries like Turkey, which has a Customs Union with the EU but nothing similar with the United States; EFTA countries Switzerland, Norway, Iceland and Liechtenstein, with related arrangements with the EU; and NAFTA members Mexico and Canada.[22] The issue of "open architecture" also has great resonance for Ukraine, Moldova and Georgia, with which the EU has signed Deep and Comprehensive Free Trade Agreements, and whose stability and prosperity is linked to U.S. interest in a Europe whole and free.

Another variant might be for the United States and the EU to negotiate new or additional WTO-compatible agreements. There is some precedent for this option as well. For instance, since Chile could not accede to NAFTA, the United States negotiated a separate bilateral arrangement.

Whatever modalities are chosen, after the agreement is concluded the two parties should be proactive about making "open architecture" real.

Addressing Concerns of Poorer Countries

A related consideration has to do with how the United States and the EU approach poorer countries. Much depends on the way the two handle the multiple trade agreements that each has with third countries and regions. They would do well to send an early signal that the TTIP is about common efforts to open markets by harmonizing their

---

[21]See http://eur-lex.europa.eu/legal-content/EN/TXT/?uri=uriserv:OJ.L_.2007.134.01.0001.01.ENG#L_2007134EN.01000401, especially points 8 and 9 of the Memorandum of Conversations.

[22]Both have free-trade agreements with the EU, but Mexico's agreement is rather rudimentary. The EU-Canada CETA agreement, while not yet ratified, is already generating questions about its relationship to TTIP. See Colin Robertson's chapter in this volume.

current hodgepodge of trade preference mechanisms for low-income African countries.[23]

Sub-Saharan Africa, the poorest region in the world, accounts for a minuscule 2% of world trade. This marginalization of the region is holding back its development at a time when its economic governance is rapidly improving. Sub-Saharan Africa needs generous access to developed consumer markets to spur investment in labor-intensive export sectors that can spark growth and contribute to its successful economic transformation.

Both the United States and the European Union give trade preferences for (some) products from (some) countries in sub-Saharan Africa. The EU provides duty-free and quota-free access to its markets for all products—but only to the 27 least-developed countries in the region. It also offers less generous access to former colonies through preferential deals. The U.S. scheme benefits 40 of the 48 countries in the region, but excludes key agricultural products (such as cotton) that African countries can produce competitively. These schemes may look good on paper, but they are actually underutilized because of their administrative complexity and outdated rules. Local content requirements are too high, and the rules of origin required for product eligibility were created decades before the development of today's value chains, which involve many countries specializing in fragmented tasks. Moreover, the United States and the EU use different methods to define origin, forcing exporters to cope with a myriad of rules.

It will be difficult to justify or implement a North Atlantic deal in which the participants have differing rules for developing countries. What foreign policy interest is served, for example, if the EU and the United States provide different access to Kenya's products? In addition, once a Transatlantic Marketplace is in place it will make no sense to have differing access arrangements for companies from third countries. The United States and the European Union could gain considerable political advantage while following through on the logical conse-

---

[23]See K.Y. Amaoko, Daniel Hamilton and Eveline Herfkens, "A Trans-Atlantic Deal for Africa," *The New York Times*, May 7, 2013, http://www.nytimes.com/2013/05/08/opinion/global/A-Trans-Atlantic-Deal-for-Africa.html?_r=0; for greater detail see the chapter by Eveline Herfkens in this volume.

quence of their own negotiations by harmonizing their trade preference schemes for sub-Saharan Africa, either as part of or as a complement to their partnership pact.

The scheme should cover all products, since excluding just a few could encompass most products that these countries can produce competitively. Rules of origin need to be relevant, simple and flexible for beneficiaries to be able to use the schemes and benefit from the growth of value chains. Such value chains have virtually bypassed the region so far, but they hold considerable potential for less-developed African countries. It is much easier for these countries to develop capabilities in a narrow range of tasks than in integrated production of entire products or processes.

Updating these rules to the realities of 21st century production networks is long overdue. WTO negotiations on clarifying rules of origin are likely to take decades; the United States and the EU could do something together now. As an interim solution the European Union and the United States could recognize each other's origin regime. If an import is eligible for preferential treatment in America, it should be also in Europe, and vice versa. By acting now, the United States and the European Union would also demonstrate that TTIP is about opening markets rather than diverting trade.

Exploiting the Full Potential of a Living Agreement

Finally, given TTIP's sheer scope and ambition, governments should reconsider whether an ambitious transatlantic effort of this type should be limited to a "single undertaking" or traditional trade negotiation, whereby nothing is really agreed until all issues are agreed. The United States and the EU should instead forge and implement agreements wherever possible, without allowing contentious issues to block areas of agreement. Too many past attempts to open the transatlantic market have failed because of these issues. At the same time, the framework needs to recognize that the U.S. and EU economies are so integrated that many of the remaining barriers and distortions are deeply embedded in their respective legal, policy and political structures, and their resolution may not necessarily fit effectively into the negotiating structure of a single, all-encompassing transatlantic agreement. Such issues should not be allowed to deadlock agreement where agreement is possible. Instead, mechanisms devised under the "Living Agreement" should be used to engage regulators, legislators and other stakeholders in areas that will require more extensive work.

Conclusion

TTIP is ambitious. It will be tough to conclude. But the potential payoff is high, and the geostrategic impact of such an agreement could be as profound as the direct economic benefits. If leaders on both sides of the Atlantic grasp the moment, America's first "Pacific President" and his EU partners may well become best known for having refounded the Atlantic Partnership. If they do not, then issues of failing trust and confidence, so visible today, will continue to eat away at the relationship like termites in the woodwork.

Chapter 1

The Strategic Significance of TTIP

Charles Ries

In 2013 the United States and the European Union began negotiation of the "Trans-Atlantic Trade and Investment Partnership," or TTIP, arguably the most significant U.S./Europe-focused economic growth initiative since the Marshall Plan. Like the Marshall Plan before it, TTIP is a "strategic" move to strengthen U.S.-European relations for the long term, just as much as a means to accelerate economic growth.

Not a New Idea

The idea is not a new one. In the early 1990s, the dissolution of the Soviet Union and the fall of the Berlin Wall—and the Maastricht Treaty's creation of a dynamic European Union out of the "euro-sclerotic" European Community that preceded it—led thinkers and statesmen to consider whether a similar initiative ought to be taken in the transatlantic relationship.

The United States had just completed the North American Free Trade Agreement (NAFTA) with Canada and Mexico, and the United States and the European Union had collaborated in the successful conclusion of the Uruguay Round of trade negotiations, creating the World Trade Organization in the process. With the end of the Cold War, it was reasonable to worry whether NATO would continue to be as relevant to the central security objectives of the United States and European nations, and whether it would continue to be the glue to bind together the United States and Europe.

Fittingly, it was two *foreign* ministers—Britain's Malcolm Rifkind and Germany's Klaus Kinkel—who were among those who prominently proposed in 1995 the negotiation of a Trans-Atlantic Free Trade Agreement (TAFTA) to eliminate tariffs and other economic barriers across the Atlantic, thereby complementing NATO and more closely tying together the U.S. and European economies.[1]

The Kinkel and Rifkind proposals ignited a short but intense debate among foreign policy and economic elites on both sides of the Atlantic as to the viability of a TAFTA. Some said that a TAFTA would be both "too small" and "too big." Too small in that tariff barriers were already so low that they do not matter, and too big in that so many sensitive vested interests would be affected that it would not be worth the political capital to undertake it.[2]

In retrospect, it is clear that the TAFTA vision was too much trade liberalization too soon after the Uruguay Round in a strategic environment that was itself too uncertain. European farmers were worried that European agriculture had been mortally wounded by the WTO's embrace of bindings on agricultural trade barriers; subsidy battles raged (e.g., over aircraft); and both the U.S. and the EU trade communities were focused on emerging economies as sources for export growth.

Also, U.S. and European policymakers feared that a regional, preferential trade agreement between the two largest economic areas (representing two-thirds of global GDP at the time) would seriously undermine the rules-based multilateral trade system that had been created with the WTO. Some thought a TAFTA might lead emerging markets to create similar agreements among themselves, damaging U.S. and European trade interests more than would be gained by the elimination of modest (between 3-4% on a trade weighted basis) tariffs across the Atlantic. In any case, economists on both sides of the Atlantic pointed out that barriers resulting from different regulatory approaches constituted far more serious barriers to trade than tariff levels.[3]

---

[1]"Remember NAFTA? Well, Here Comes TAFTA," *Businessweek*, May 7, 1995 (http://www.businessweek.com/stories/1995-05-07/remember-nafta-well-herecomes-tafta-intl-edition).

[2]Siebert, Horst; Langhammer, Rolf J.; Piazolo, Daniel, "TAFTA: Fueling Trade Discrimination or Global Liberalization?" Kiel Institute for World Economy, Kiel Working Papers, No. 720, 1996 (http://www.econstor.eu/bitstream/10419/869/1/193325942.pdf).

[3]Ibid., pp. 15-16.

As a result, when in December 1995 the United States and the European Union declared the "New Transatlantic Agenda," the two entities pledged increased attention to regulatory and other barriers to trade, but stopped short of deeper commitments to a regional trade agreement.[4]

Politically, new projects for transatlantic cooperation quickly emerged: the stabilization of the Balkans after the break-up of Yugoslavia (and the wars that followed), and the enlargement of the European Union and NATO, designed to incorporate the vulnerable states of central Europe newly free from the Warsaw Pact looking for allies and a prosperous economic future.

Other priorities captured the imagination of the United States and the European Union over the following fifteen years. The European Union did enlarge, from the 15 member states of 1995 to 28 member states in 2013. NATO also enlarged, despite strident opposition from the Russian Federation. The terrorist attack of 9/11 in New York, and subsequent attacks in Madrid and London, brought about transatlantic cooperation in counter-terrorism. The U.S. intervention in Afghanistan became a NATO mission.

In the trade world, momentum to build on the Uruguay Round was stymied first by determined opposition in developed countries (especially the violence at the Seattle WTO ministerial of 1999) and then, following the launch of a new multilateral round of trade negotiations at Doha in 2001, by skepticism concerning the merits of negotiated trade liberalization in major emerging economies, especially India and Brazil. So even though the United States and EU had not pursued a TAFTA, many of the feared adverse effects happened anyway.

At the "coal face" of the U.S.-EU relationship, various efforts were made to deal with the regulatory barriers to trade even without a free trade agreement. A series of limited mutual recognition agreements were reached, although only in sectors with clear support from industry and regulators. In 2007, with White House leadership and support,

---

[4]"The New Transatlantic Agenda," December 5, 1995 (http://uscu.usmission.gov/new_transatlantic_agenda.html). The New Transatlantic Agenda did envision a "joint study" of "ways of facilitating trade in goods and services and further reducing or eliminating tariff and non-tariff barriers," but such a study was never undertaken.

a Transatlantic Economic Council (TEC) was set up to bring regulators, trade and finance ministry officials together to tackle U.S.-EU barriers to trade and investment.[5] It had limited success.

What's Different Now?

As the "post" post-Cold War era began, U.S. and EU economic relations looked ripe for new attention and ambition. As an early sign of the "rebalancing" to Asia, in 2010 the United States had agreed with a number of Pacific Basin trading partners (including several countries that had existing free trade agreements with the United States) to the negotiation of a "Trans-Pacific Partnership" (TPP) to include "high-standard" trade and investment liberalization provisions. Some began to ask why not do something similar with Europe, which has been mired in a slow growth recovery from the great recession of 2008-09? After all, the United States and the European Union represent nearly half of global GDP and 30% of world trade, exchange goods and services worth $2.7 billion every day, and have directly invested more than $3.7 trillion on both sides of the Atlantic.[6]

At the U.S.-EU Summit in November 2011, the United States and the European Union announced the creation of a High Level Working Group to examine the feasibility of a thorough-going high-standard trade and investment liberalizing agreement. (Such a study group also preceded the decision to proceed to negotiate NAFTA.)

With evidence mounting of European interest in the idea of a high-standard, trans-Atlantic economic liberalization agreement, U.S. Secretary of State Hillary Clinton encouraged the idea in remarks at a Brookings Institution conference in November 2012.[7] In his State of the Union Address in January 2013, President Barack Obama embraced the idea, saying "[a]nd tonight, I'm announcing that we will launch talks on a comprehensive Transatlantic Trade and Investment Partnership with

---

[5] http://www.state.gov/p/eur/rt/eu/tec/c33255.htm.

[6] *Final Report, High Level Working Group on Jobs and Growth*, February 11, 2013 (http://www.ustr.gov/about-us/press-office/reports-and-publications/2013/final-report-us-eu-hlwg), p. 1.

[7] Secretary of State Hillary Clinton, "The U.S. and Europe, a Revitalized Global Partnership," Address at the Brookings Institution, November 29, 2012 (http://www.brookings.edu/events/2012/11/29-transatlantic-clinton).

the European Union—because trade that is fair and free across the Atlantic supports millions of good-paying American jobs."[8]

In conjunction with the State of the Union address, the High Level Working Group released its report.[9] The report identified the following as "potential options" for an agreement:

- "Elimination or reduction of conventional barriers to trade in goods, such as tariffs and tariff-rate quotas.

- Elimination, reduction, or prevention of barriers to trade in goods, services and investment.

- Enhanced compatibility of regulations and standards.

- Elimination, reduction, or prevention of unnecessary 'behind the border' non-tariff barriers to trade in all categories.

- Enhanced cooperation for the development of rules and principles on global issues of common concern and also for the achievement of shared global economic goals."[10]

Following a period of consensus-building in Europe, the European Union approved a mandate for negotiation of a TTIP in June 2013, although the French sought to make their position clear that "cultural" industries were to be off-limits for liberalization.[11] The negotiations formally started in July 2013.[12] In addition to the agenda proposed by the High Level Working Group, the negotiators have committed themselves to find new rules on issues of global concern such as protection of intellectual property and treatment of products and services provided by state-owned enterprises.

---

[8]President Barack Obama, "Remarks by the President in the State of the Union Address," February 13, 2013 (http://www.whitehouse.gov/photos-and-video/video/2013/02/12/2013-state-union-address-0-transcript).

[9]*Final Report, op. cit.*

[10]*Final Report, op cit,* p. 1.

[11]http://www.english.rfi.fr/americas/20130613-france-will-veto-eu-us-trade-talks-if-culture-included.

[12]"Readout from the First Round of TTIP Negotiations, July 8-11, 2013." (http://www.ustr.gov/trade-agreements/free-trade-agreements/trans pacific partnership/readouts/round1)

The Strategic Advantages of TTIP

A TTIP would in the first instance benefit the U.S. and EU economies. A number of economic analyses have been published, with varying assumptions (mainly about how thoroughly abolished the mainly regulatory non-tariff barriers would be). Britain's Centre for Economic Policy Research estimated economic gains for the EU as a whole amounting to €119 billion per year (after a 10 year phase-in) and €95 billion a year for the United States.[13] A Bertelsmann Foundation study estimated even bigger gains, predicting economic gains to the United States from a deep liberalization scenario equal to 13.4% of GDP, with benefits for major EU member states in the 5-9% of GDP range.[14] Even if the impact is on the lower end of the scale, it is still important and can help support growth and investment trends in the two largest (but most mature) global markets.[15]

If successfully concluded and ratified by the U.S. Congress and the European Council, however, the TTIP would be much more than a trade agreement. It would mark the beginning of a new period for U.S.-European cooperation, one less dependent on only the NATO connection. Among the strategic advantages of the trade and investment deal are the following:

It would provide a new sense of purpose for transatlantic relations, at a time when the United States has stated its intention of rebalancing to Asia and is reducing its military presence in Europe. These two developments are causing some Europeans to question the commit-

---

[13]Francois, Joseph, Miriam Manchin, Hanna Norberg, Olga Pindyuk, and Patrick Tomberger, *Reducing Trans-Atlantic Barriers to Trade and Investment: An Economic Assessment*, London: Centre for Economic Policy Research, 2013, p. vii.

[14]Felbermayr, Gabriel, Benedikt Heid, and Sybille Lehwald, "Transatlantic Trade and Investment Partnership: Who Benefits from a Free Trade Deal?" Global Economic Dynamics, *Bertelsmann Stiftung*, June 17, 2013 (http://www.bertelsmann-stiftung.de/cps/rde/xchg/SID-EEC0BA1A-B12DB94A/bst_engl/hs.xsl/nachrichten_116768.htm).

[15]However, some TTIP opponents question the value of such economic impact analyses and emphasize the modest size of the expected economic gains. See, for example "TAFTA Studies Project Tiny Economic Gains, Assume No Costs from Gutting Safeguards," Eyes on Trade, *Public Citizen*, December 18, 2013 (http://citizen.typepad.com/eyesontrade/2013/12/tafta-studies-project-tiny-economic-gains-assume-no-costs-from-gutting-safeguards.html).

ment of the United States to Europe. Continued sharp reductions in European defense budgets are leading some Americans to question Europe's commitment to NATO. TTIP would also counteract impressions in some quarters of a supposed "decline of the West."

TTIP would provide significant economic stimulus at a time of slow growth. Although eliminating tariffs with the United States would reduce EU revenues and vice versa, eliminating quotas and more compatibility in standards and conformity assessment would be revenue-neutral or might reduce expenses.

TTIP would provide a positive political context in which to attack the most significant impediments to trade and investment among the two entities: the inconsistent regulatory approaches to product regulations, including health, safety and environmental regulation. Despite occasional assertions[16] to the contrary, the United States and the European Union both have strong regulatory systems to protect consumers and the environment. These systems have been developed over many years and in many cases grounded in legislation. Inconsistent and incompatible regulatory approaches impose substantial burdens on industry and consumers. They are even more evident in the absence of tariffs. Different product designs, package labeling, dimensions and a host of other details increase production and marketing costs. So in addition to the elimination and reduction of specific regulatory barriers to be provided for in the agreement itself, TTIP would provide momentum towards regulatory convergence.

Already, the U.S. Department of Agriculture has announced that the Animal and Plant Inspection Service will modernize U.S. bovine spongiform encephalopathy (BSE)-related import requirements to be more consistent with international regulations; in other words the United States will now accept EU beef and bovine product exports.[17]

---

[16]See, for example, "Trade Deal to Undermine Health, Environmental Standards," Institute for Agriculture and Trade Policy, Washington http://www.iatp.org/documents/trade-deal-to-undermine-health-environmental-standards-sthash.zoXrwUw1.dpuf; Cole Stangler, "The Next Corporate Friendly Trade Pact," *These Times* (http://inthesetimes.com/article/16044/ttip_the_next_corporate_friendly_trade_deal/).

[17]Kara Sutton, "TTIP Negotiations: A Summary of Round 2," B Brief, Bertelsmann Foundation, December 6, 2013, p. 2.

Within Europe, a successful TTIP can counteract some of the malaise and hostility towards Brussels-based institutions in member states beset by slow growth and austerity, or skeptical of population movements. For Europeans, TTIP can genuinely be said to be more feasible to negotiate by the European Union rather than as separate nation-states.

TTIP would open the door for greater direct participation in transatlantic trade by small and medium-sized enterprises. While multinational companies currently account for large proportions of trans-Atlantic imports and exports (in 2013, 61% of U.S. imports from the European Union, and 31% of EU imports from the United States, were categorized as trade between "related parties"[18]), there would be new scope for exports from, and innovation by, smaller companies. The Internet opens the possibility of successful international marketing by small start-ups offering goods and services, just as it has disrupted many other industries. If niche companies in Milwaukee can start to see market opportunities in Düsseldorf without tariff barriers and associated paperwork, Americans and Europeans will come to realize how much they are linked in a broader transatlantic marketplace.

To realize such a potential small business boom, the agreement will need to be crafted to encourage this type of trade. One way would be to enlarge the *de minimus* allowance for goods shipped by post or small parcel shipment service. That would allow web-based sellers to send packages of goods valued below a threshold (such as U.S. Customs' $800 personal exemption allowance) to any buyer (business-to-business or business-to-consumer) in the United States or the European Union without more paperwork or regulatory burdens than those demanded for shipments within their respective borders.[19] With elimination of tariffs, there would be no reason to worry about valuation and collection of duties. Obviously there would still be categories

---

[18]Daniel Hamilton and Joseph Quinlan, *The Transatlantic Economy 2013: Annual Survey of Jobs, Trade and Investment Between the United States and Europe*, Washington: Center for Transatlantic Relations, Johns Hopkins University, p.2 (http://transatlantic.sais-jhu.edu/ publications/books/Transatlantic_Economy_2013/TE2013 volume 1.pdf).

[19]As proposed by (an interested party): Drucker, Michael L. (Executive Vice President and Chief Operating Officer, Fed EX), "The Transatlantic Trade & Investment Partnership: Achieving the Potential," Testimony to the U.S. Senate Committee on Finance, October 30, 2013.

of goods that could not be traded this way (such as firearms, tobacco or spirits) due to regulatory or safety concerns.

Encouragingly, the United States and the European Union have already agreed[20] to include a chapter on small and medium enterprises in the final agreement. They have created a negotiating group on the topic. And the International Trade Commission is completing a study requested by the U.S. Trade Representative on EU trade barriers that disproportionately affect small and medium-sized enterprises.[21]

Many other issues must also be resolved in the negotiations. In agriculture, while progress has been made in reining-in subsidies and both the United States and the EU are becoming more globally competitive, commodity sectors are distorted by a variety of current and historical support programs. Long phase-in periods may be needed to eliminate tariff and quota barriers completely. Whether and how a TTIP will apply to the large financial service sector will also be a major issue. American regulators are opposed to harmonization of prudential bank regulation, since U.S. law is more demanding that comparable EU requirements. And as noted earlier, the French are strongly opposed to any liberalization that might put their support for their cultural sectors (including film and other media) at risk.

Impact on the Wider World

A TTIP may serve to bring the major emerging markets back to the table in the WTO, offering in the process much expanded market access. In the Pacific, China is newly interested in becoming involved

---

[20]As the EU's lead negotiator Ignacio Garcia Bercero stated on December 20, 2013, "... I would like to highlight that it will be critical that the TTIP achieve real and include benefits for the small and medium enterprises, and that this is reflected throughout the agreement, but also in a specific chapter within SME related issues." Transcript (as delivered) "Chief Negotiators Dan Mullaney and Ignacio Garcia Bercero Press Conference Following the Third Round of Transatlantic Trade and Investment Partnership (TTIP) Talks December 20, 2013" (http://www.ustr.gov/about-us/press-office/press-releases/2013/December/TTIP-Third-Round- Press-Conference-transcript).

[21]United States International Trade Commission, Investigation No. 332-541, "Trade Barriers that U.S. Small and Medium-Sized Enterprises Perceive as Affecting Exports to the European Union," http://www.usitc.gov/secretary/fed_reg_notices/332/332_541_notice 07252013sgl.pdf.

in the Trans Pacific Partnership. The advent of NAFTA had a bit of this competitive liberalization impact on the final stages of the Uruguay Round.

TTIP will need to be approached with an eye towards the interests of key trading partners of the European Union and the United States. Under the terms of its Customs Union with the EU, Turkey would be required to provide duty-free access to U.S. goods without gaining corresponding duty-free treatment from the United States. This anomaly could be corrected by a side agreement between the United States and Turkey. The United States would gain much in the application of TTIP's expected enhanced investment provisions and new services access to Turkey; Turkey would gain from tariff reductions for its exports to the United States and participation in the processes designed to de-conflict regulatory systems. The European Union also has free trade agreements with Switzerland, Norway and Iceland where similar benefits of enlargement would be easily achieved.

Mexico and Canada, partners of the United States in the NAFTA, already have separate free trade agreements with the European Union, although the EU's free trade agreement with Canada is not yet ratified. If these agreements were made compatible with a TTIP, a truly seamless Atlantic market would be created.

The United States and the European Union should state now that they will consult with these close trading partners as the TTIP is being negotiated. If TTIP succeeds, the partners would intend to follow with an effort to conform all these agreements (in trade coverage and rules of origin, in particular) to reduce distortions and generalize the benefits.

Do the Right Thing, After Exploring the Alternatives

When I was assigned to the U.S. Mission to the EU as the Counselor for Economic Affairs in the early 1990s, it struck me that all the "good news" seemed to be on the political side of our relationship. At the time, we were working closely with the European Union to build a new Europe "whole and free," tackling emerging threats and better coordinating our initiatives in multilateral organizations. However, when it came to economics and trade, the U.S.-EU relationship was much more contentious. We had seemingly intractable disputes about bananas, beef, aircraft subsidies, mobile phone technologies, mergers, television programming and a host of other issues.

Today, some of these differences and disputes persist. Yet in the context of structural changes in the global economy and the unsettled, acute security challenges in the Middle East and (more distantly) in the Asia-Pacific regions, we have come to realize how "strategic" a strong, balanced and deep *economic* relationship can be for the transatlantic community. In the years ahead, if we grasp the opportunities, the good news indeed can emerge from the economic relationship.

The United States and the European Union may fail to achieve their highest ambitions, but the stage is set for a major step forward with a TTIP, which, by the "Monnet method" under which the EU itself was built, may set the stage for further liberalization. A TTIP, complementing NATO and the other longstanding political and alliance links between us, will be the foundation for a strengthened "Atlantic Basin" that can confidently turn to the Pacific, the Middle East or other challenges in the decades ahead. That will be the strategic significance of TTIP.

Chapter 2

The Geopolitical Implications of TTIP

Robert D. Hormats

There are a multitude of reasons why a well-constructed and well balanced Transatlantic Trade and Investment Partnership, or TTIP, is greatly in the interest of both the United States and Europe. Many of these are in the economic realm. The United States and Europe are each other's largest trading and investment partners. And while neither has enjoyed robust growth recently, although U.S. growth is now picking up, even a small amount of trade liberalization, improvement in trans-Atlantic regulatory consistency and harmonization of standards-setting practices can have a significant positive impact on transatlantic commerce and on job creation. This is because even a small percentage point increase in the enormous volume of commerce that flows between our continents can produce big increases in trade. Moreover, if the United States and EU can agree on common regulations, consistent standards setting practices, mutual recognition of tests in certain areas, recognition of science-based decisions on key trade-related procedures etc. in important areas, we will together be in a stronger position to encourage other nations or entities to adopt them, giving our companies and workers further benefit. If we want to be on the winning side of globalization we need proactive trade policies that improve global rules and we can best do that together. If we fail, other will seize the opportunity—and we will be divided against one another and as we face the world.

Related to this are the geopolitical implications of TTIP. It is difficult to imagine a clearer wakeup call for closer U.S.-European cooperation than recent events in Ukraine. With the United States having devoted more attention to Asia of late, and now being diplomatically drawn into the Middle East in a variety of ways, all the "tapering" in Washington did not come from the Federal Reserve. Europe received relatively little attention both in relative and absolute terms. And on Europe's side, there were those who argued that it did not need the US as much in part because the security threat had diminished and in part because Europe itself was devoting more attention on the economic front to Asia's growing markets and to attracting Asian investment. All this should have changed as the result of Russian actions in Ukraine—and other activities on its western border. But has it?

It is surprising and disappointing that the importance of enhanced economic relations as a way of enhancing U.S.-European solidarity in the wake of these actions has not been greater. Both sides speak of it and write about it, but the level of political commitment and the full-throated endorsement of TTIP as a priority seem a bit underwhelming. President Obama made a key point in arguing for firm resolve regarding support for Ukraine when he addressed European Youth on his March 2014 visit to Brussels. He warned about how badly the world would see us "If we defined our interests narrowly..." in these circumstances. The danger with TTIP, I fear, is that if we define our interests too narrowly in these talks, if we might fail to see the broader benefits of TTIP. And the rest of the world, beginning in Moscow but not ending there, would conclude that a moment when the a US and Europe should find a way to overcome historic but often relatively obscure trade differences,

The goal in these negotiations then should first and foremost be a sound agreement that can stand the test of scrutiny on economic ground on both sides of the Atlantic, because without that it will not get the popular or legislative support it needs for passage. But there are ways of defining interests very narrowly and ways of defining them more broadly—and in the current geopolitical environment it is imperative that both sides recognize the necessity of the latter. American and European leaders need to make this point more forcefully and effectively than they have in the recent past.

Let's look at the stakes in historic terms. The glue that held the United States and Europe together for many years, particularly during the Cold War, was NATO. To put it succinctly, it kept American forces in Western Europe and Soviet forces out. Most Americans and Europeans supported that US presence. The United States maintained substantial troop strength in Western Europe for decades and a significant number of European members of the Alliance maintained substantial troop levels for several decades as well; large portions of the populations on both sides of the Atlantic understood why the Alliance was there and how vital it was.

Trade and investment, of course, were vitally important parts of the broader political and security relationship. Initially supported by the Marshall Plan and then by the Kennedy Round of trade negotiations and growing private sector engagement in transatlantic commerce and investment, the economic dimension of the relationship supported the recovery of Western Europe. That in turn enabled it to become a stronger ally of the United States in the Cold War and reduced its vulnerability to internal instability, from time to time fomented by extremist groups. Some of these were purely internal in nature; others were supported by the Soviet Union or those sympathetic to its views or ideology.

Europe's economic recovery also boosted American growth and job creation; imagine, for a moment, how much weaker the American economy would have been during this period had Europe not recovered its economic strength and how much greater the American defense budget would have been had there been constant political instability in western Europe, fewer resources generated there to defend themselves and more domestic instability inviting external intervention of various types.

Now we find ourselves in a very different world. The Cold War ended over two decades ago. So did the existence of the entity known as the Soviet Union. And today younger generations of Americans and Europeans have little or no knowledge of what NATO is or why it is there—much less of the critical role it played in protecting Europe's freedom for several decades, setting the stage for a united Germany in a united Europe and addressing wars in other parts of the continent, for instance the Balkans, after the Cold War ended.

In addition, there are growing pressures in the United States to reduce America's global engagement in various parts of the world and cut back on military presence overseas. A recent poll by the Pew Research Center indicated that 52% of Americans asked responded that the "US should mind its own business internationally and let other countries get along the best they can on their own." Among those who felt this way, 28% said they did because of the cost of foreign involvement. Add to this the growing pressures to reduce budgetary expenditures for all programs, including the military. America's NATO forces are unlikely to be exempt from these pressures.

In Europe, major cuts in forces have already taken place. These began well before the financial crisis—for budgetary reasons and because of less overall public support in a great many countries in Europe for maintaining a large military establishment. This drop in public support can for the most part be attributed to the end of the Cold War and significant reluctance to engage in military activity elsewhere in the world. The financial crisis and the resulting additional budget cuts to restore fiscal stability have further sharpened that trend. Moreover Europe's already costly social welfare system requires growing sums of money—and further competes with military budgets for resources. Former U.S. Defense Secretary Robert Gates described American concerns about this situation in his June 2011 Farewell Speech in Brussels; he warned that budget cuts in Europe would lead to a two-tiered NATO, which in turn could cause the United States to pull back from support for the transatlantic security relationship.

There is a strong argument for sustaining a well-prepared NATO; recent events relating to Ukraine vividly and tragically illustrate the need. It is also important to meet contingencies in other parts of the world where the joint military help of the United States and Europe is required—as an indication that the United States and Europe are prepared to meet threats to stability, to vulnerable populations and to shared interests in a unified way. Recent actions in Libya fell into this category.

But it is also true that the European Union today encompasses a much wider range of countries than those in Europe that are members of NATO, and that for the vast majority of Europeans, economic prosperity and stability—particularly the creation and sustainability of jobs—are the top priority. The same sentiment is true for the vast majority of Americans. Indeed, significant numbers of Americans oppose greater military involvement abroad while at the same time support various types of international economic engagement. They do the latter because they recognize that it produces domestic economic benefits. In the same Pew study cited above, 66% of Americans said that U.S. involvement in the global economy was a good thing because "it exposed the US to new markets and opportunities for growth. It must be said, however, that many Americans do not have a positive attitude toward trade agreements; many in weighing the pros and cons of these see them as harmful to jobs and wages at home because they augment competition from foreign companies, which in the eyes of many has greater negative weight that the positive weight of potential export benefits.

TTIP comes into play here because success in these negotiations—an agreement that both sides see as balanced and expanding mutual opportunity—would demonstrate a transatlantic response to the concerns of tens of millions of Americans and Europeans who have been adversely affected by the recent economic crisis and thus are keenly and urgently focused on economic priorities. The added trade and investment will provide tangible economic benefits on both sides of the Atlantic. It will remind both Americans and Europeans of how much the relationship between the two continents benefits their common economic interests today—just as it was in the post-WWII era. That in turn can underpin support for the kinds of broader security and U.S.-EU political ties embodied in NATO and in various other non-alliance, but similarly important, political ties.

This connection is of crucial geopolitical importance for American and Europeans alike. Global competition today is not simply about goods and services. It is also about which nations' economic and political models or systems are most responsive to their citizens needs and serve the interests of societies seeking to prosper in this rapidly changing global economic environment. The most powerful message that can be sent by countries that value their democratic systems and believe in the power of market economies to produce growth and advance living standards for their people is to demonstrate that their political and economic systems are successful in producing positive results.

By advancing trade and investment opportunities across the Atlantic, the EU and the United States, which share so many values and interests, can demonstrate to their own citizens and to the world that they are capable of taking the bold decisions—particularly needed now in light if events in Ukraine—that enable stronger and less impeded economic ties between them to improve the lives of their citizens. To the extent they succeed, leaders on both sides will enjoy increased popular support for other types of transatlantic collaborative action, outside the economic realm. And both Europe and the United

States will be more credible in advocating policies and institutions in other parts of the world that are consistent with their own values and practices.

It would be naïve, of course, to believe that this will mean instant agreement to work together on every security or political challenge the United States or members of the EU face, or that success will have a decisive influence on the attitudes of other nations or their responsive to American and European suggestions for policy reform. But a more dynamic and visible set of economic ties has at least the potential to enhance cooperation on some matters in the geo-political realm and their success in a world in which other nations are concerned about Europe and the United States playing a diminished role. Success in these negotiations can play a significant role in dispelling these attitudes.

In the more specific arena of trade and investment, the ability of Europe and the United States to agree upon common rules, regulations, standards and approval processes in areas where differences currently impede commerce and business operations can not only produce bilateral benefits but also provide a template for other negotiations in other parts of the world and for forging a common position for encouraging other countries or regional groupings to adopt such rules or practices. This would give the United States and EU together a considerably greater chance to shape global rules on trade and investment than would be the case if the two were divided.

In that latter circumstance, other nations or groups of nations would be in a much stronger position to influence the process and to force their national preferences on others. Or there would be a more "Balkanized" system of global rules that would lead to problems for American and European companies, which would have to produce goods and services to comply with several sets of national or regional standards—one for their home market and others for a series of other markets.

This is not merely an economic consideration. Joint European-American leadership in setting the global trade rules enhances prospects that trade regionalism—which can lead to both economic and political frictions—over time can be slowed and that nations and regional groups can gradually converge around more broadly agreed rules and practices. This can in turn produce a wide range of geopolitical benefits by countering the kinds of trade fragmentation and disputes that weaken cooperation on a broader range of issues.

All told, there are a wide range of geopolitical as well as economic benefits to be derived from a successful TTIP. Although the results of these negotiations must first and foremost pass the test of economic soundness and mutual benefit on both sides of the Atlantic, considerable weight must also be given to the geopolitical benefits. During the recent financial crisis we all learned how much economic disruption on one side of the Atlantic affects the other. And the last seventy years should have taught us that prosperity in Europe and the United States is mutually reinforcing.

In much the same way, history makes it quite clear that year in and year out virtually every international political and security challenge the United States has faced has seen Washington call on America's European friends and allies first and to rely on Europe far more than on any other group of nations. Likewise, in times of crisis or need, Europe consistently looks to the United States first. And no two groups of nations have closer ongoing collaboration on security, intelligence and political matters than the NATO partners of Europe and North America.

It is vitally important that all these connections and patterns of cooperation continue. But they cannot be taken for granted, and require constant efforts on both sides to ensure that they are strengthened and that electorates and various social groups understand their value and see tangible benefits from this relationship. Benefits must be seen and felt on Main Street America and in what President François Mitterrand often referred to as "La France Profonde." While the Cold War is thankfully over, the threats to the security and political interests of Americans and Europeans continue in Europe and in many other parts of the world. A successful TTIP that demonstrably boosts job-creating trade and investment in the United States and Europe will further underscore to Americans and European the direct economic value of close transatlantic ties to them and will provide reinforcement of broader and vitally important political and security ties as well. And it will send a powerful message to the rest of the world that the United States and Europe are able to take decisive steps forward at a time when solidarity between them is greatly needed to revitalize their own economies, to reinforce their cooperation and to play a collective leadership role in promoting their values on the global stage.

Chapter 3

Parsing TTIP's Geopolitical Implications

Charles A. Kupchan

American and European negotiators are hard at work trying to bring to a successful conclusion negotiations over the Transatlantic Trade and Investment Partnership (TTIP). The primary motivation behind this effort is to boost economic growth on both sides of the Atlantic. Amid a prolonged economic downturn, American and European policy makers are searching for measures capable of stimulating growth and creating jobs. Structural constraints in Europe and political gridlock in the United States make a free trade agreement one of the more attractive options available for achieving these objectives.

Although its economic impact is the chief driver behind TTIP, the pact would also have important geopolitical consequences. These geopolitical consequences are, however, not well articulated by policy makers. Moreover, the scholarly literature provides indeterminate findings as to the geopolitical implications of increased economic interdependence. Some studies indicate that commercial interdependence facilitates political cooperation and geopolitical stability, suggesting that TTIP, if successfully concluded, may be an important source of transatlantic solidarity.[1] Other studies are more circumspect about the strategic implications of interdependence, finding little evidence that economic integration on its own is an important contributor to geopolitical stability.[2] High levels of interdependence among Europe's major powers did little to stave off World War I. In similar fashion, commercial and financial flows between China and Japan appear to have little effect on dampening geopolitical rivalry. From this perspective, policy makers and analysts alike should be careful not to overstate TTIP's political and strategic implications.

---

[1] See, for example, Edward D. Mansfield and Jon C. Pevehouse, "Trade Blocs, Trade Flows, and International Conflict," *International Organization*, Vol. 54, No. 4 (Autumn 2000), pp. 775-808.

[2] See, for example, Charles Kupchan, *How Enemies Become Friends: The Sources of Stable Peace* (Princeton: Princeton University Press, 2010).

The goal of this chapter is to explore the likely geopolitical impact of TTIP. It argues that a transatlantic free trade pact would have significant geopolitical implications. In particular, TTIP, by creating jobs and stimulating growth, would help revitalize the Western democracies and advance the prospects for the West's reclamation of political and strategic purpose. As the distribution of global power continues to shift from the West to the "rising rest" in the years ahead, it is essential that the Atlantic democracies remain a strong and effective anchor of liberal values and practices. TTIP has an important role to play in guiding the West out of its economic and political malaise, thereby enabling it to serve as the anchor of liberal democracy in a world headed into an era of profound change.

This essay will also argue, however, that TTIP could potentially have significant geopolitical downsides. The more ambitious and exclusive the "club" constituted by the Atlantic democracies, the higher the barriers to entry, and the less likely it is that emerging powers will want or be able to play by Western rules. In this sense, TTIP could exacerbate dividing lines between the West and rising states. Another risk is that the Atlantic democracies come to view TTIP as a substitute for strategic partnership and turn to commercial ties to serve as the West's binding glue. To do so would be a dangerous mistake. The strength of commercial ties across the Atlantic notwithstanding, the Western democracies must ensure the continued viability of NATO and work to uphold their historic commitment to collectively shoulder geopolitical burdens. TTIP cannot serve as a substitute for NATO.

The chapter begins by exploring TTIP's geopolitical upsides. It then examines the pact's potential downsides and illuminates the need for sobriety about its positive geopolitical effects. The analysis is not meant to argue against TTIP. On contrary, the pact's overall economic and geopolitical effects are definitively positive. Nonetheless, it is important for the Atlantic democracies to proceed with eyes wide open.

The Positive Geopolitical Effects of TTIP

The Weakening of the Liberal Order

Europeans and Americans have been the world's trend-setters for the last two centuries; together, they forged the liberal international order that has accompanied the onset of a globalized and interdependent world. The long run of the West's material and ideological hegemony is, however, coming to an end. The liberal international order erected during the West's watch will face increasing challenges in the years ahead. The collective wealth of the developing world has surpassed that of the developed West, limiting the capacity of the advanced industrialized economies to set the terms of a rules-based order. In addition, expectations that the end of the Cold War would readily clear the way for the global spread of liberal democracy have proved illusory. State capitalism is alive and well in China, Russia, Vietnam, Saudi Arabia, and a host of other countries. In most of Central Asia, the Middle East, and Africa, democracy has yet to put down firm roots. Emerging powers that are liberal democracies, such as India and Brazil, seem at best ambivalent about aligning themselves with the West. It no longer seems plausible, as many analysts have predicted, that emerging powers, democracies and non-democracies alike, will readily embrace the rules of the liberal order on offer from the West.[3]

The weakening of the liberal international order erected during the West's watch is in part the product of immutable processes of global change. Globalization is speeding the diffusion of power, reallocating wealth and productive capability from the Western democracies to the developing world. This diffusion of power is leading to growing ideological diversity rather than ideological convergence. China, Russia, Saudi Arabia and other non-democracies are bent on resisting, not embracing, the rules of the road associated with *Pax Americana*. In the Middle East, the Arab awakening has strengthened political Islam, challenging the West's preference for demarcating a boundary between the realms of politics and religion. Participatory politics may well be arriving in the region. But, if so, the Middle East will be following its own path to modernity—not one that portends ideological convergence with the West.

The West's diminishing ability to anchor a liberal international order is a product not only of a relative decline in its share of global wealth and the rise of emerging powers that are challenging prevailing

---

[3]See, for example, Francis Fukuyama, *The End of History and the Last Man* (New York: Free Press, 1992); and G. John Ikenberry, *Liberal Leviathan: The Origins, Crisis, and Transformation of the American World Order* (Princeton: Princeton University Press, 2011).

norms. In addition, the West is experiencing a stubborn economic downturn coupled with unprecedented political polarization and dysfunction. As a consequence, the Western model has lost some of its luster. Domestic difficulties have also hampered the conduct of statecraft and prompted an inward turn at the very moment that the West needs to be fully engaged in the task of managing peaceful change.

This downturn in the West's fortunes represents a new and surprising development. The West's economic success and political stability have long given it global allure and encouraged developing nations to emulate the Western path of development. Indeed, initial confidence about the likely universalization of a liberal international order was predicated upon a process of convergence that would over time bring the developed and developing world into institutional and ideological alignment. The Western model worked; developing nations would follow it, convergence would take place, and they would gradually integrate into the Western liberal order.

But the prospects for such convergence have considerably dimmed. Western economies are struggling, America's political system is in a state of virtual paralysis, and the European Union is experiencing its own crisis of governance resulting from the populism and discontent stoked by the eurozone crisis. In the meantime, China's brand of state capitalism has produced impressive results. Beijing has brought hundreds of millions of Chinese citizens out of poverty, and the Chinese economy weathered the recent financial crisis far more successfully than Western economies. Chinese firms and development agencies are increasingly present throughout the developing world, undercutting Western efforts to tie aid and trade to liberal reforms. At least for now, the Western model no longer has a monopoly on the aspirations and plans of nations seeking to better their economic and political futures. The Chinese model is not about to overtake the world. But its success indicates that multiple versions of modernity will be vying with each other in the marketplace of ideas.

The West's economic and political troubles have also produced a diminishing appetite for strategic engagement abroad. For the foreseeable future, the EU will be focused on recovering financial stability and repairing the project of European integration; Europe will rarely be looking beyond its own neighborhood. America's elected representatives and its public are weary and wary after more than a decade of war in the Middle East. Washington will be choosing its fights very carefully, as made clear by President Obama's insistence on keeping America's distance from the civil war in Syria. His caution is reflected in the electorate. A recent Pew opinion survey revealed that over 50% of Americans believe the United States should "mind its own business internationally."[4] Americans are tired of distant wars and want investment in schools and bridges in Kansas, not in Kandahar. Partisan polarization is also taking a toll on American statecraft. The shutdown of the U.S. government in the fall of 2013 prevented Obama from attending key summits in Southeast Asia, undercutting his effort to "pivot" U.S. policy toward Asia. A U.S. trade delegation heading to Brussels for negotiations on TTIP also had to cancel due to the shutdown. From Japan to Saudi Arabia, foreign governments are preparing themselves for a scaled-back American role in their respective regions.

Pax Americana has rested on the readiness of the United States and Europe to provide public goods and serve as the global providers of last resort. Recent economic and political trends within the West appear to be limiting its capacity and willingness to continue playing that role, suggesting that the liberal order erected after World War II will suffer from lack of enforcement and maintenance.

Revitalizing the West

There are multiple sources of the West's political weakness, but the primary cause is its lackluster economic performance. The wages of America's middle class have been stagnant for the better part of three decades. Today, the real income of the average American worker is lower than it was twenty years ago. In the meantime, the wealth of the nation's top earners has increased markedly, making inequality in the United States the highest in the industrialized world. European workers have suffered a similar fate. Even in Germany, the EU's top performer, the middle class has shrunk by some fifteen percent. Youth unemployment in the EU's southern tier hovers around forty percent.

---

[4]Pew Research Center for the People & the Press, "Public See U.S. Power Declining as Support for Global Engagement Slips, http://www.people-press.org/2013/12/03/public-sees-u-s-power-declining-as-support-for-global-engagement-slips/.

These economic conditions are at the heart of the political dysfunction plaguing the West. In the United States, inequality and economic insecurity are bringing back to life ideological cleavages not seen since the New Deal era, contributing to polarization and paralysis. Across the EU, economic duress is leading to the renationalization of political life, turning electorates against the project of European integration and eating away at the EU's social solidarity.

It is on this front that TTIP can make its most important geopolitical contribution. Estimates vary, and the economic impact of TTIP would depend upon the details of the pact. Nonetheless, TTIP promises to significantly boost jobs and growth on both sides of the Atlantic.[5] In light of political constraints in the United States and the prospect of continued austerity in Europe, a transatlantic free trade pact offers one of the few options available for creating jobs and stimulating growth. By reducing non-tariff barriers and harmonizing regulations, TTIP would also help advance the extension of the single market within the EU, thereby promoting further economic gains.

With growth rates in the United States already picking up, economic expansion in the EU is particularly important and urgent. A perilous gap has opened up between EU elites and the European "street." Elites are fashioning plans for a fiscal and banking union, steps vital to stabilizing the euro. However, electorates are meanwhile growing ever more doubtful of the merits of deeper integration. Indeed, with the sole exception of Germans, European electorates are increasingly skeptical of the prospect of ceding more power to Brussels. According to a recent Pew poll, "positive views of the European Union are at or near their low point in most EU nations, even among the young, the hope for the EU's future. The favorability of the EU has fallen from a median of 60% in 2012 to 45% in 2013. And only in Germany does at least half the public back giving more power to Brussels to deal with the current economic crisis."[6]

Reviving economic growth is critical to re-legitimating the EU in the eyes of European voters—just as a robust recovery is essential to

---

[5]According to one official assessment TTIP could create 400,000 jobs and boost the EU economy by €119 billion a year and the American economy by €95 billion.

[6]"The New Sick Man of Europe: The European Union," Pew Research Center, May 13, 2013, p. 1.

restoring the efficacy of democratic institutions in the United States. It is particularly important that economic recovery on both sides of the Atlantic advantage middle class workers and not just the elite. Improving the living standards and restoring the optimism of average Americans and Europeans are top priorities. Replacing economic dislocation and uncertainty with improving fortunes and confidence is the *sine qua non* of efforts to reclaim political efficacy and purpose among the Atlantic democracies. An economic and political recovery advanced by TTIP would also demonstrate to voters the merits of openness and international engagement as opposed to protectionism and retreat.

TTIP would thus constitute an important step forward in renewing the West's political vitality and enabling it to continue serving as the anchor of liberal democracy amid a world in change. So too would the West's recovery refurbish the allure of the Western model, of particular importance as emerging powers chart their courses in the years ahead.

Regionalism and Free Trade

The era of global trade liberalization appears to be on hold, if not over. The Doha round of negotiations shows few signs of moving forward. The United States, which has since World War II been the shepherd of successive rounds of liberalization, is no longer ready to play that role; globalization and the accompanying loss of manufacturing jobs have sapped Washington's enthusiasm for ambitious free trade initiatives. It is worth noting that over the course of the George W. Bush and Barack Obama administrations, Washington has concluded only three minor trade pacts—with South Korea, Colombia, and Panama. The growing influence of emerging economies with trade agendas different from those of the industrialized West, such as India and Brazil, also contributes to stalemate in the Doha round.

Under these circumstances, bilateral and regional trade agreements for now offer the only available means of advancing trade liberalization. Moreover, TTIP looks to be one of the most politically viable pacts currently under consideration. Tariffs across the Atlantic are already quite low. The United States and the EU have economies at relatively similar levels of development, meaning that legislatures in both the United States and Europe would not see TTIP as an agreement that would lead to outsourcing and job loss. A transatlantic free trade pact thus represents "low-hanging fruit" when it comes to advancing the cause of trade liberalization.

Should TTIP be successfully concluded, it has the potential to have positive knock-on effects in other regions. A transatlantic pact could help set global standards, setting an example that other trade groupings might follow as they seek to advance liberalization. So, too, might a transatlantic free trade agreement trigger action in other regions. Concerned about being left out of the gains in commerce and prosperity enjoyed by the United States and the EU, China, Brazil, and other emerging economies might undertake their own efforts to liberalize trade. Such "competitive regionalism" appears to have been a factor in the 1990s as trade groupings in a host of different regions—including Europe, South America, North America, and the Asia-Pacific—all made significant steps forward. With global liberalization stalled for the foreseeable future, regional pacts may well be the only game in town. And TTIP has significant potential to get the ball rolling.

If a transatlantic free trade area does indeed help advance economic integration in other regions, the benefits promise to be geopolitical as well as economic in nature. As the United States and Europe become less able and willing to provide public goods, and as international institutions (such as the G-20 and the UN Security Council) become more unwieldy due to increases in membership, regional institutions may well have to pick up the slack. It could well be that bodies like ASEAN, the Gulf Cooperation Council, the African Union, and the EU become ever more important contributors to providing governance and security in their respective regions. Developing the capacities of regional institutions is thus an important investment in future stability. To the degree that TTIP helps encourage integration and capacity building in other regions, it would have geopolitical benefits well beyond the Atlantic area. As Europe's own history has demonstrated, economic integration can usefully serve as the leading edge of political integration.

Commercial Contributions to Atlantic Solidarity

The strategic partnership between the United States and Europe is likely headed into a less activist phase. NATO is in the process of winding down its presence in Afghanistan—a mission costly and inconclusive enough to make it very unlikely that the alliance would again undertake an operation of similar scope. NATO's intervention in Libya was more effective in military terms, but the consequences for stability in Libya have raised doubts about the mission's merits. Moreover, only a handful of NATO countries contributed to that mission, raising questions about the readiness of alliance members to participate in future missions. Germany, in particular, seems to be turning inward; Berlin's appetite for shouldering geopolitical burdens is on the wane. So, too, is defense spending in Europe being substantially reduced. NATO is likely to remain open for business and continue to serve as the Atlantic community's venue of choice of strategic cooperation. But it is poised to decline in activism and political salience.

TTIP may well help offset the strategic drift that is likely to set in across the Atlantic. American and European leaders are both expending significant political capital on TTIP, bringing the transatlantic partnership back into the limelight. After TTIP negotiations were launched, some commenters suggesting that the United States was "pivoting back" to Europe. The negotiations themselves are regularly bringing together American and European diplomats as well as stimulating dialogue among top representatives from the private sector. These activities are raising the public profile of the transatlantic partnership and propagating a narrative of mutuality and commonality. Should TTIP succeed in creating jobs and growth on both sides of the Atlantic, publics will reap the concrete benefits of transatlantic cooperation and their appreciation of the partnership will rise accordingly.

TTIP thus has the potential to consolidate the political bond between the United States and Europe at a time when security ties may be loosening. However, as the next section indicates, it would be illusory and perhaps dangerous to see increased commerce as a substitute for strategic partnership.

Cautionary Reflections on the Geopolitical Effects of TTIP

Although TTIP promises to have positive geopolitical effects, these effects should not be overstated. Moreover, the pact may have significant geopolitical downsides. Most importantly, it has the potential to widen the political gap between the West and emerging powers.

Conventional wisdom foresees the universalization of the rules-based order erected during the West's watch; emerging powers are expected to embrace this order as they modernize. However, today's rising states, as those that have come before them, have made clear that they aspire to change the existing order in ways that advantage their interests and ideological preferences. The BRICS grouping, for example, is intended to provide Brazil, Russia, India, China, and South Africa a forum that serves as an alternative to other institutional venues, which they see as dominated by and serving the interests of the Western democracies.

TTIP could well exacerbate this problem. The higher the standards set by Western rules, the less likely it will be that rising states are willing and able to play by those rules. The nature of the trade agreement being negotiated between the United States and the EU is unique to economies at similar stages of development that already enjoy relatively free commerce. To be sure, membership in the WTO and other, more generic, forms of governing international commerce have helped foster convergence toward common rules. But TTIP, precisely because of the far-reaching scope of the agreement, could do the opposite: stratify, if not, fragment a rules-based order.

TTIP also has the potential to foster a political backlash among emerging powers. The maintenance of a rules-based international order in the years ahead will depend upon the ability of the Atlantic democracies to work with emerging powers, not just with each other. Nonetheless, TTIP deepens integration within the Atlantic community, not more broadly. In this sense, it could communicate to the rest of the world a fortress mentality among the Atlantic democracies. Emerging powers may see the agreement as another instance of the West focusing on the West rather than on the well-being and prosperity of the broader international community. TTIP thus could make more elusive one of the paramount strategic tasks ahead in the years ahead—fashioning consensus between the Atlantic democracies and emerging powers on the terms of new rules-based order.

This potential downside does not offset TTIP's main upside—its ability to help revitalize the West economically and politically. That revitalization is an urgent priority; only if the West reclaims its sense of political purpose will it be able to effectively engage rising powers and play a guiding role in managing international change. Nonetheless, the Atlantic democracies should keep in mind TTIP's potential to widen the political and perceptual gap between the West and the "rising rest." The Atlantic community should therefore take compensatory steps, such as addressing head-on the need to work with emerging powers to forge a new rules-based system.

Finally, Western elites and publics alike must guard against the view, recently articulated by a former high-ranking U.S. official, that "TTIP is the new NATO." As discussed above, a free trade pact between the United States and Europe would help give new political salience to the transatlantic partnership and engender transatlantic solidarity. Nonetheless, deepening commercial engagement is no substitute for strategic partnership. The realms of commerce and security tend to be relatively compartmentalized. If the United States and Europe drift apart as security partners, commercial interdependence is unlikely to be affected. At the same time, however, commercial interdependence will not be able to forestall strategic drift. TTIP should be pursued for its own sake, not as a means of compensating for a waning strategic partnership.

Accordingly, even if TTIP is successfully concluded, the Atlantic democracies cannot afford to let their strategic bond atrophy. That means that EU member states will have to step forward on the defense front, doing more to pool their assets and coordinate their policies—especially in an era of enduring constraints on defense spending. The United States will certainly have to demonstrate patience as the EU seeks to recover from the renationalization spawned by its financial crisis. But it should nonetheless continue to stress the need for the EU to aggregate its will and capability on foreign and defense policy. In the meantime, Washington should ensure that NATO receives adequate political and material support—even as the focus of US defense policy tilts toward East Asia. Deepening NATO's training and partnership programs outside the Atlantic area would help maintain political support for the alliance at a time when most of the security challenges facing its members lie well beyond Europe's borders.

Conclusion

TTIP represents a golden opportunity to expand jobs and growth on both sides of the Atlantic. Economic renewal promises to help foster political renewal, better enabling the West to remain a solid anchor of liberal values and practices—of paramount geopolitical importance as power shifts from the developed to the developing world. At the same time, TTIP cannot offset strategic drift among the Western allies, an issue that will have to be addressed on its own terms. Moreover, even as the Atlantic democracies deepen their ties to each other, they must keep their eyes on the prize and work with emerging powers, democracies and non-democracies alike, to fashion a new rules-based system for the twenty-first century. The Atlantic democracies already constitute a peaceful and prosperous community. The challenge ahead is helping to extend that accomplishment to the rest of the world.

Chapter 4

TTIP: Don't Lose Momentum!

Thomas Straubhaar

The world economy is challenged by a brand new trend: for the first time since decades the wheels of globalization are turning more slowly.[1] It looks like the post-World War II era of global economic liberalization is coming to a halt and perhaps, in the worst case, to an end. In many countries, the further opening up of national markets has gotten stuck. Protectionism has returned as a political strategy.[2]

In earlier times, the World Trade Organization (WTO) would have worked as a counterweight to the temptation of national authorities to rebuild impediments to free international exchange of goods and factors. Its aim is "to open markets for trade" ("where countries have faced trade barriers and wanted them lowered").[3] However, the WTO has lost momentum recently. After a decade of negotiations it has not able to reach more than just the absolute minimum and to avoid the worst scenario: the complete collapse of the Doha Round of multilateral trade negotiations.

The weak compromise on trade facilitation reached by WTO members in the very last minutes of their meeting in Bali in December 2013, after many years of debate, was nothing more than a symbolic bypass operation. It helped the WTO to survive but did not cure the causes of the malady: with about 160 WTO member countries, the world economy has become too complex to find a common single solution.

---

[1] In 2012–2013 world trade grew below the long-term average rate (measured in volume terms, i.e., adjusted to account for inflation and exchange rate movements). In the period from the 1980s to 2008, the growth rate for world trade was around twice that of world gross domestic product (GDP), but in 2012 the ratio of world trade growth to world GDP growth fell to around 1:1 See World Trade Organization (WTO), *World Trade Report 2013*, Geneva 2013, p. 21.

[2] "In recent years the trend to greater openness has been replaced by an enthusiasm for building barriers—mostly to the world's detriment. ... Policymakers have become choosier about whom they trade with, how much access they grant foreign investors and banks, and what sort of capital they admit. They have not built impermeable walls, but they are erecting gates," "The Gated Globe," *The Economist*, Special Report, October 12, 2013.

[3] See: http://wto.org/english/thewto_e/whatis_e/who_we_are_e.htm.

33

The United States and the European Union (EU) have been the parents of the global multilateral order in the post-World War II era. Now they see this period of Western dominance in setting the rules of the game coming to an end. The emerging economies are hardly or even not at all willing to accept rules established more or less unilaterally by the West, as was the case in the past. They want to bring in their points of view, their values, norms and interests.

As a consequence of the shift in (economic) power from the West to other world areas in the last decades, the speed and development of global multilateralism have slowed down. Strong initiatives for further worldwide liberalization rounds are not in sight. This tendency is not favorable for economic growth, which reduces the options to make use of existing economic potentials in the transatlantic area. Therefore, for the United States and the EU the search for alternatives to global multilateralism is a wise strategy. And a regional transatlantic agreement might be the best they could find. It is politically feasible and improves economic welfare. That is the key message of this chapter.

The first section of this chapter shows that globalization—the economic offspring of global multilateralism—has lost momentum recently because public, and thus political, attention has shifted from the economically positive growth effects of liberalization to the much more controversial issues of distributing the benefits and costs of globalization. The second section argues that a comeback of global multilateralism dynamics within the WTO will not taken place for years to come. Therefore, regionalization might be a good substitute for global multilateralism. The third section presents the Transatlantic Trade and Investment Partnership (TTIP) as a concrete example of the new paradigm of regional multilateralism. The final section draws the conclusion that TTIP would lead to stronger growth, more jobs and higher standard of livings—firstly and directly in the United States and Europe but lately and indirectly also in other world areas.

Sand in the Wheels of Globalization

The reasons for the recent slowdown in the globalization process are basically the same as those that stimulated globalization in the post-World War II period: changes in transaction costs. Most of the time in the last decades, political and technological changes have gone hand in hand stimulating and strengthening each other. Technological improvements have been allowed to cross national borders easily and cheaply, and to expand national markets to a global dimension. Simultaneously, political arrangements like the creation of international institutions—the General Agreement on Tariffs and Trade (GATT—later the WTO) or regional agreements like the European Union (EU) or the North American Free Trade Area (NAFTA)—have liberalized international activities. They curtailed economic nationalism and restricted beggar-thy-neighbor policies. Thus, politics allowing international business, and technology enabling international exchange, have together been the parents of globalization.

More recently, transaction costs for doing global business have rather increased than further declined. Obviously enough, globalization follows the iron economic law of diminishing returns: the further it has gone already, the smaller the additional benefits will be in the future. On the other hand marginal costs are rising: the more global business is organized, the more complex it will become. In total, globalization might be close to optimal scale that would balance further benefits of a global division of labor with the additional costs of coordinating actors from different and diverse places.

Even more important, perhaps, is that the wind of politics has recently shifted. "Globalization and its discontents"[4] has received more attention than the economic benefits of worldwide open goods and factor markets.[5] Several reasons might have been responsible for this shift:

1. Even if globalization has led to improvements in the standard of living for the mass of people worldwide, the gap between the rich and the poor did not narrow, it has become larger.[6] The distance between advanced and developing economies when they are taken as two aggregates have converged but there are still millions of people in some of the poorest coun-

---

[4]Joseph E. Stiglitz, *Globalization and its Discontents* (New York/London: Norton, 2002).

[5]Jagdish Bhagwati, *In Defense of Globalization* (Oxford: Oxford University Press, 2004).

[6]See Branko Milanovic, "More or Less?", *Finance & Development*, September 2011, vol. 48, no. 3, pp. 6-11 and—older but broader—Lant Pritchett, "Divergence, Big Time," *Journal of Economic Perspectives*, 1997, vol. 11, pp. 3-17.

tries whose incomes have remained almost stagnant for more than a century and divergence increased between the richest people in the world and the very poorest, despite the broad convergence of average incomes.[7] Some countries have caught up indeed. But others have been rocked by political crisis and social turmoil. As a consequence, the distributional and social aspects of globalization have gained more attention. This can be seen anecdotally in the protests against globalization by the so-called "occupy movement" or turmoil in Brazil, Venezuela, Thailand or China.

2. The period of globalization has gone hand-in-hand with an increasing demand for natural resources and raw materials. In many regards this has led to increasing environmental costs, climate change and the question whether the consequences of economic globalization are sustainable or lead to pollution, global warming and ecological catastrophes, mostly and especially to the costs of poorer people who are not able to finance mitigation and protection measurements.

3. The financial market crisis of 2008/2009, with its attendant, long-lasting tremendous economic consequences, has acted like a culminating point in the last decade. It was eye opener and game changer alike, bundling all the criticisms against globalization, sorrows and fears, broken promises and disappointed hopes. It has slowed down the dynamics of economic development in the emerging economies of Southeast Asia and Latin America. And it has led to increasing unemployment figures around the world. That is why most governments had to protect domestic markets through all kind of policies (fiscal, trade and monetary policies). The United States and the EU had their stimulus packages, India imposed local-content requirements on government purchases of information and communications technology and solar-power equipment, and Brazil urged local firms to buy more from local companies.

---

[7]Kemal Dervis, "Convergence, Interdependence, and Divergence," *Finance & Development*, September 2012, vol. 49, no. 3, pp. 11-14.

4. The recession following the financial market crisis provoked a return of protectionism. "After two decades in which people, capital and goods were moving ever more freely across borders, walls have been going up, albeit ones with gates."[8] In particular, the exchange rate has been re-detected as the most important weapon in a blazing currency war (look at the Japanese case as the probably most prominent example).[9] A devaluation of the currency to protect the domestic economy is a much more powerful instrument of protectionism than any import duty. And it promotes exports stronger than any export subsidy.

All in all, the pace of globalization has slowed down recently. The share of internationally traded goods and services relative to total world production and foreign direct investment has failed to attain pre-crisis levels. This is especially true for global capital flows, which have collapsed from $11 trillion in 2007 to barely a third of that figure in 2012.[10]

Similarly, the current volume of world trade lies in the post-crisis period well below the long-term trend from 1990 to 2008.[11] The world economy is now less globally connected than in 2007. The 2012/2013 ratio of world exports of merchandise and commercial services has not yet reached the peak value of 2008.[12]

It has become obvious that "Globalization is neither inevitable nor irreversible."[13] "Governments increasingly pick and choose whom they trade with, what sort of capital they welcome and how much freedom they allow for doing business abroad."[14] The consequence of the

---

[8]"Gated Globe," *op. cit.*

[9]Of course the tremendous crash of the national currencies—like in Argentina or Turkey in spring 2014—has gone much below a currency war strategy and was fueled by the expectation of a recovery in the United States and further turmoil (as described above) in some emerging markets.

[10]"Gated Globe," *op. cit.*

[11]*World Trade Report 2013, op. cit.*, p. 23.

[12]Ibid., figure 1.3.

[13]Ibid., p.5.

[14]"Gated globe," *op. cit.*

return of protectionism is simple: the pressure on globalization leads to pressure on global multilateralism.

Regional Multilateralism as a Substitute for Global Multilateralism

The United States and Europe were the pioneers of a liberal world economic order after World War II. They believed in the iron laws of international trade. According to them, opening up national markets allows for welfare enhancing specialization, international division of labor and an efficient reallocation of production factors. Consequently, both the United States and the EU promoted the establishment of a global multilateral system. first via the GATT and later the WTO, with a universal, uniform and equal treatment of countries (and people).

There is no doubt that the United States and the EU would still benefit from a further liberalization of international trade in goods and services, investments and business activities within a global multilateral system. A world economy with lower or no artificial exchange barriers would reduce transaction costs for international trade, investments and migration. However, after the failure to speed up the further development of the WTO in Bali in 2013, the dynamics for finding a new global multilateral economic order will be slowed down for many years. Further major improvements to the WTO are not in sight.

The rising political and economic power of emerging markets questions the concept of global multilateralism. Liberalization and globalization are challenged by new powers outside the transatlantic rim. Many more players with many more different interests have joined the worldwide game of international exchange of goods and factors. Homogeneity is gone. Heterogeneity is in. And this challenges the global multilateral approach that has been regulating international economic activities since World War II. Universality, uniformity and equal treatment of states cannot be attained anymore.

New approaches for a reanimation of further liberalization of international activities are needed. This is in the interest of all countries. Economic theory can easily demonstrate that national borders and walls are costly—also for the economy that should be protected. And empirical evidence confirms the negative impact of protectionism on growth and employment. The experience of the last decades clearly shows a definite statistical link between freer trade and economic growth.[15]

However, if the first best solution (i.e. a global multilateral system that aims to remove barriers to trade in goods, services and factors) is politically not feasible, a second best solution (where at least some countries remove restrictions on international activities) might be a wise compromise. Removing borders and opening up national markets to some but not every country is not as good as a world without trade restrictions, but it is better than a world with nationally protected markets.[16]

The idea of "second best" solutions is the midwife of a liberalization arrangement between the United States and the EU. An agreement should be easier between these two partners than among many (i.e. about 160 WTO members)—especially since the two partners share many basic values and have a long historical common background.

While global multilateralism would generate the largest economic benefits of globalization (at least theoretically), regional multilateralism has a higher likelihood to convey the benefits faster in practice. It follows the pragmatic judgment that some liberalization is better than no liberalization, independent of whether it is regional or global.

For the United States and the EU, the only viable way to further develop a liberal economic order is to start small rather than big and to go regional rather than global. Further steps to liberalize international economic activities have to be negotiated among a few rather homogeneous partners with a broad range of common goals and not

---

[15]"Protection ultimately leads to bloated, inefficient producers supplying consumers with outdated, unattractive products. In the end, factories close and jobs are lost despite the protection and subsidies. If other governments around the world pursue the same policies, markets contract and world economic activity is reduced. One of the objectives that governments bring to WTO negotiations is to prevent such a self-defeating and destructive drift into protectionism." (http://wto.org/english/thewto_e/whatis_e/tif_e/fact3_e.htm).

[16]The concept of "second best solutions" was developed in the 1950s. See James Edward Meade, *Trade and Welfare* (Oxford: Oxford University Press, 1955), and Richard G. Lipsey and Kelvin Lancaster, "The General Theory of Second Best," *Review of Economic Studies*, vol. 24, no. 1 (1956–1957), pp. 11-32. More recently, Dani Rodrik, "Second Best Institutions," *American Economic Review*, vol. 98, no. 2 (2008), pp. 100-104, has applied the concept to argue that appropriate institutions for developing countries are "second-best" institutions— "those that take into account context-specific market and government failures that cannot be removed in short order. Such institutions will often diverge greatly from best practice."

among heterogeneous actors with different interests. Regional, not global, multilateralism is the answer to the changes in the world economy, including the political and social reluctance to accept the outcomes of the new globalization.

TTIP as a Pragmatic Approach to Further Liberalization

In June 2013, President Barack Obama, European Council President Herman Van Rompuy, and European Commission President José Manuel Barroso launched the Transatlantic Trade and Investment Partnership (TTIP). The founders of the TTIP idea have left open how far they would like to go by integrating economically Europe and the United States. They have simply declared that the United States and the EU aim to deepen their bilateral relationship, assert their trade policy leadership, and advance a rules-based system of global economic governance that reflects their shared values and interests.

As TTIP indicates, the focus lies in a trade and investment agreement between the United States and the EU that aims to remove trade barriers (both tariffs and non-tariff trade barriers [NTBs] like differences in technical regulations, approval procedures and recognition of technical standards and product admission) in a wide range of economic sectors in order to facilitate the buying and selling of goods and services between the United States and the EU.

TTIP's goal is to eliminate all impediments in bilateral trade in goods and investments according to the principle of origin. For the trade in services, the aim is to obtain improved market access and to address the operation of any designated monopolies and state-owned enterprises.

TTIP would amalgamate the world's two largest economies. And of course it would resolve concerns of the EU about the fact that the United States is engaged in talks about a Trans-Pacific-Partnerships (TPP).[17] Measured in purchasing power parity, the United States and

---

[17]The TPP is currently being negotiated among twelve countries (i.e. United States, Canada, Mexico, Peru, Chile, New Zealand, Australia, Singapore, Malaysia, Brunei, Vietnam, and Japan). The threat to the EU is that TPP could generate serious trade diversion effects for EU economies.

the EU together are responsible for almost 40% of global GDP, for almost 60% of worldwide foreign direct investment,[18] and for one-third of worldwide trade in goods and services.[19]

The expected economic effects of TTIP are well analyzed in theory.[20] They can be summarized as: a) trade creation, b) trade expansion and c) trade diversion effects. While the first two impacts are clearly positive the third one is negative. Trade diversion leads to discrimination against third countries. As a result, there might arise a feeling of unfair treatment culminating in anti-liberalism tendencies or even an aversion to the Western economic order.

The expected economic effects of TTIP are tremendously positive.[21] According to a CEPR study, the annual GDP growth stimulus could reach up to 0.5% of GDP (about 160 billion U.S. dollars) for the EU, and 0.4% of GDP (about 130 billion U.S. dollars) for the United States. A Bertelsmann Foundation study estimates that at least a total of 750,000 new jobs would be generated in the United States alone.

---

[18]See United Nations Conference on Trade and Development (UNCTAD), *World Investment Report 2013*, (Geneva: 2013).

[19]*World Trade Report 2013*, op. cit.

[20]As an example see the seminal book by Jacob Viner, *The Customs Union Issue* (New York: Carnegie Endowment for International Peace 1950), newly edited and with an introduction by Paul Oslington, (New York: Oxford University Press, 2014). Especially in the 1950s the theory of customs union has been established further. The *World Trade Report 2011* presents an exhaustive survey about the literature and the recent state of the art in both theory and empirics (see World Trade Organization (WTO), *World Trade Report 2011*, Geneva, 2011).

[21]The economic consequences of TTIP have been analyzed broadly in a study by CEPR (see Centre for Economic Policy Research (CEPR): *Reducing Trans-Atlantic Barriers to Trade and Investment* (project leader Joseph Francois), London March 2013) and in several articles by the Ifo-Institute in Munich (see Gabriel J. Felbermayr, and Mario Larch, "The Transatlantic Trade and Investment Partnership (TTIP): Potentials, Problems and Perspectives," *CESifo Forum* vol. 14, no. 2, June 2013, pp. 49-60). Some of the Ifo results have been published together with the Bertelsmann Foundation (see Gabriel J. Felbermayr, Benedikt Heid and Sybille Lehwald, *Transatlantic Trade and Investment Partnership (TTIP): Who Benefits from a Free Trade Deal? Part 1: Macroeconomic Effects.* Bertelsmann Foundation (Gütersloh, 2013) Available at http://www.ged-project.de/studies/study/who-benefits-from-a-transatlantic-free-trade-deal/). And finally there is a Bertelsmann study that evaluates the job effects of TTIP; see: Tyson Barker, Anne Collett, and Garrett Workman, *TTIP and the Fifty States: Jobs and Growth from Coast to Coast.* Atlantic Council of the United States, the Bertelsmann Foundation, and the British Embassy in Washington, Washington 2013.

The optimistic expectations are caused by the fact that the United States and the EU are each other's most important trade partners. Both regions have similar cost and production structures, similar levels in economic development, deep political relations and strong cultural similarities. Therefore the reduction of trade frictions could help to reallocate more efficiently production factors (especially capital i.e. firms and their production sites) and to make use of comparative advantages, economies of scale and joint research activities to develop new technologies.

TTIP would generate significant economic gains on both sides of the Atlantic. Because the levels of tariffs between the United States and the EU are already very low, the dismantling of non-tariff barriers between both regions has a much bigger influence on the growth process and on the employment rate than the dismantling of tariffs. The CEPR study simulates the potential impact of a TTIP in a couple of liberalization scenarios.[22] In one "limited" scenario, where only tariffs are eliminated (98% of all tariffs), a growth stimulus of 0.1% is projected for the EU per year ($31.7 billion) and 0.04% per year ($12.5 billion) for the United States. However, in a second "comprehensive/ambitious" scenario, where 98% of all tariffs and 25% of NTBs on goods and services and 50% of procurements non-tariff barriers are abolished, the benefits would be much higher. Annually, the EU's GDP is estimated to increase by 0.48% ($158.5 billion) and U.S. GDP by 0.39% ($126.2 billion).

The general view is that 70-80% of TTIP benefits will come through aligning U.S. and EU approaches to regulation. The goal will be an agreement stating that, while domestic rules and regulations across many sectors may be different in the United States and European Union, there is no need for harmonization. Rather, both sides can identify sectors in

---

[22]CEPR and Ifo as well base their economic assessments on a simulation of a computable general equilibrium (CGE) model. The two studies differ with respect to aggregation. The Ifo study models 126 separate countries, but adopts a macroeconomic single-sector perspective. The CEPR study works with 10 regions, but adopts a multi-industry perspective. To obtain a detailed explanation of the model used by the CEPR respectively by the Ifo Institut see Francois, et al. (2013: 21-25 and 105-112) respectively Felbermayr, et al. (2013: 57-63 and 140-147) and for a methodological comparison between the CEPR and the ifo-studies see Gabriel J. Felbermayr and Mario Larch, "Transatlantic Free Trade: Questions and Answers from the Vantage Point of Trade Theory," in *CESifo Forum*, vol. 14 (2013), no. 4 (December), pp. 16-17.

which they recognize the essential equivalence of each other's regulatory systems. This would be a cost-saving measure and help avoid duplications or contradictions across the Atlantic. To do this successfully, however, equal treatment independent of nationality will be crucial. Domestic and foreign certifications have to be treated the same way.

However, and for the long run even more importantly, TTIP would also allow the United States and EU to define basic standards for open flows of investment, which could have a major effect on opening growth markets elsewhere in the world.[23] This is of special importance because investment will drive the dynamics of transatlantic activities, just as trade drives the transpacific relationships. TTIP would allow U.S. and European firms to construct their value chains more efficiently, better profit from larger economies of scale and scope, and to be able to exchange ideas, skills, and firm-specific knowledge more easily across the Atlantic. This would not only bring some static costs savings, as in the case of trade. It would also allow for new forms of producing and processing that stimulate growth rates and not just cost levels.

The United States and the EU together are already by far the most important players in the world's financial markets. "Achieving convergence or common regulatory standards could leave in its wake an explosion of growth in these markets."[24] If successfully done, TTIP could become the rule-setter for new global standards—with a first advantage for the United States and the EU.

While the effects of TTIP might become tremendously positive for the United States and the EU, the consequences for the rest of the World would be rather negative in the short run. Especially those countries which are geographically close to the United States or to the EU and countries which already maintain free trade agreements with the United States and/or the EU or countries which have a high trade volume with either one or both of the transatlantic giants, must expect to lose trade flows through the trade diverting effects of a TTIP in the short run.

---

[23]See also: Bernard Hoeckman, "Business and Transatlantic Trade Integration," in *CESifo Forum*, vol. 14 (2013), no. 4 (December), pp. 28-32.

[24]Jim Kolbe, "Alice in Trade-Land: The Politics of TTIP," GMF Policy Brief, February 2014, p. 3.

The simulation studies confirm the intuitive expectation that trade diversion would matter a lot for neighbors or strong trading partners. TTIP would lead to strong trade-diverting effects within the NAFTA area. Trade with Canada and Mexico would fall substantially and consequently per capita income in the neighboring countries would fall dramatically (in the worst case by about a total of 7% for Mexico and 9.5% for Canada in the long run). But the highest declines in the trade flows would be seen between the United States and China.

However, in the long(er) run the higher growth, the additional jobs and the increase in the standard of living in the United States and the EU will lead to stronger economic relations also with the outside world.[25] Thus, TTIP will not only stimulate the U.S. and EU economies. It will also improve the economic situation of neighboring countries and the outside world in the long run.

That makes clear how crucial it is that TTIP remains open for other countries willing to accept the rules of the game of a new transatlantic order. TTIP should be an inclusionary, rather than exclusionary agreement. If TTIP establishes common standards and reduce regulatory divergences and invites other countries to join, the likelihood is high that third countries might profit and will experience a decline in trade costs and an increase in their GDP as well. Therefore, the TTIP has the chance to promote economic growth worldwide.

To lower concerns in the rest of the world that TTIP might be the end of global multilateralism, it should be open for other countries to join in principle. It should be clearly communicated to partners beyond the transatlantic area—particularly those in the Transpacific Partnership (TPP), who might be concerned that TTIP is designed to be an exclusive arrangement—that those who want to join would be able to do so.

The only precondition for joining TTIP would be the acceptance of a "TTIP Acquis Atlantique" by the date of accession. This means that joining would be an all-or-nothing decision for new members.

---

[25]Empirical evidence from existing regional trade arrangements does not show that in the past regional and global liberalization have proceeded together, they have tended to reinforce each other, the interactions have been largely positive throughout the postwar period; see the contributions in: Richard Baldwin, and Patrick Low (eds.), *Multilateralizing Regionalism: Challenges for the Global Trading System* (WTO: Geneva, 2008).

They would have to accept all TTIP norms and requirements in order to join, without any ability to negotiate changes to the TTIP Acquis.

In practice not many other countries might be willing or able to accept the "Acquis Atlantique" of TTIP without having the chance to change it according to specific national preferences. However, for the neighbors of the United States and the EU such access could be realistic. Being outsiders they would be harmed most in the short run and could profit far more by becoming a member of TTIP in the long run. Therefore for them it might be a very profitable decision to join TTIP.

Conclusion: Do It and Do It Now!

The United States and the EU should start a new liberal order quickly and economically successfully or there will be no further liberalization anymore at least for some time. They should not wait for a common global understanding of what should be done. Such a joint global agreement will not be found soon, and if there will be a compromise it is uncertain what it would look like, and it might contradict the economic interests and liberal values of the "West."

TAFTA (Transatlantic Free Trade Area), TEC (Transatlantic Economic Council) and other previous initiatives for a deeper transatlantic integration were bottom-up in nature, pushed by either single countries or with one side of the Atlantic taking the lead. TTIP, however, is top- down. It is a high priority on the agenda of both the U.S. president and the European Commission.

TTIP is the pragmatic answer of the United States and the EU to the shift from global to regional multilateralism that could be seen worldwide.[26] It is an effort to find common ground among transatlantic partners with a long common history. The EU and the United States are relatively close in their shared understanding of fundamental values like individualism, liberalism, constitutionalism, human rights, liberty, rule of law and democracy. Therefore win-win-agreements, compromises and further steps towards liberalization and an opening up of national goods, labor and capital markets might be

---

[26]For a survey of the many regional arrangements, see *World Trade Report 2011, op. cit.*

reached easier than on a global level where national interests differ much more.

TTIP follows the empirical evidence of the past that more liberalization is better than less and that regional multilateralism is better than no multilateralism. So the expectation is that TTIP is a good strategy not only for the transatlantic area but for the world economy as a whole. For that reason "countries outside the EU and the United States, especially the larger emerging economies, should fear TTIP failure rather than TTIP success."[27]

To be ultimately successful, TTIP negotiators should consider "rejecting the single undertaking approach to negotiations, where nothing is agreed until everything is agreed."[28] Instead, negotiations should start on transatlantic trade, investment and regulatory cooperation. However, they should be ready to include additional themes like financial services, energy, environmental issues or corruption. Eventually, TTIP could serve as a single economic area for all kinds of businesses. While an opting out (from the Acquis) should not be possible, an opting-in approach should be possible for countries that wish to go ahead with cooperation in certain areas.

After an optimistic start in 2013, negotiations are stuck in 2014 for several reasons:[29]

1. Genetically modified organisms: Americans might see genetically modified food as a solution to the problem of starvation, Europeans might see it as a source for new problems of and with agro-business.

2. Media ("cultural exception"): Europeans want to protect their cultural heritage against an unwanted and unbeloved "Ameri-

---

[27]Frederik Erixon, "The Transatlantic Trade and Investment Partnership and the Shifting Structure of Global Trade Policy," *CESifo Forum*, vol. 14 (2013), no. 4 (December), p. 19.

[28]Daniel Ikenson, "Fresh Ideas for a Successful Transatlantic Trade and Investment Partnership," *CESifo Forum*, vol. 14 (2013), no. 4 (December), p. 27.

[29]For recent information on the status of negotiations see The TTIP Forum at the Center for Transatlantic Relations, Johns Hopkins University School of Advanced International Studies (SAIS) http://transatlantic.sais-jhu.edu/index.htm#TTIP or the Atlantic Council (http://www.atlanticcouncil.org/blogs/ttip-action/about-ttip-action) "TTIP Action" project, each of which offer the latest news and analysis on TTIP.

canization." Americans see this goal as a (poorly disguised) demand for protection.

3. Privacy (NSA/PRISM-affair): Unless there is a common transatlantic understanding about the minimal standard of privacy protection, the European Parliament might not sign a TTIP agreement. Going forward, both sides will need to have a serious discussion about where to set the balance between security and privacy and liberty, a contentious debate which has been ongoing since 9/11. A U.S.-EU working group has been set up on the issue; both sides must use this mechanism to reach some agreement, otherwise it is more than doubtful that the European Parliament will ratify TTIP.[30]

4. Some Europeans fear that an investment agreement with the United States might become a Trojan horse allowing American companies to subvert European regulations and to gain access to the EU Single Market without having to accept European laws and standards. Opposition is especially strong with regard to labor standards ("hire and fire"), social standards (minimal protection) and environmental standards.

5. The missing authority for President Obama to sign a TTIP agreement on a "fast track" makes the negotiations very complex. As long as the Congress does not provide the President with "Trade Promotion Authority," negotiators on both sides could of the Atlantic cannot be sure whether Congress would carve up any agreement. What if the President agrees on what has been negotiated but Congress wants to change some paragraphs? How would the Europeans react? And: how does this uncertainty influence the negotiation process?

6. The May 2014 European Parliament elections and formation of a new European Commission means that for 2014 political leadership will be missing, and it is unclear who eventually will be in charge in the endgame of the negotiation process.

---

[30]See Annegret Bendiek, "Beyond US Hegemony: The Future of a Liberal Order of the Internet," in *Liberal Order in a Post-Western World* (Washington, DC: Transatlantic Academy, 2014).

Having in mind the undeniable benefits of TTIP, there is no doubt that it would be worth to overcome rapidly the difficulties and to avoid further delays.[31] The TTIP initiative comes at the right time. Globalization has lost momentum. Benefits of doing business with the emerging markets have declined and transaction costs have increased. The financial crisis has led to high unemployment rates and high public debts on both sides of the Atlantic. New impulses for growth are needed to improve prospects for employment, growth and welfare.

TTIP could spur growth, translate into millions of new jobs in the United States and Europe, and improve both earnings and competitiveness for many companies, particularly small and medium-sized enterprises on both sides of the Atlantic. However the benefits would not be restricted to the United States and the EU. They would spread out worldwide. In the long run, all countries could benefit from more prosperity in the transatlantic area. That is why TTIP should become a success, not a failure, and why TTIP should gain, not lose, momentum.

---

[31]Remarkably enough, several empirical studies have analyzed the impacts of TTIP with different methods but all come to the same positive evaluation.

Chapter 5

TTIP, Central and Eastern Europe, and Russia

Edward Lucas

President Barack Obama's speech in Warsaw in June 2014 high-lighted a new tone in transatlantic relations. For some countries of countries of central and eastern Europe, it was high time—a welcome if belated change. For others, it seems to have come too late.

In the region that was once conveniently known as "eastern Europe," the Transatlantic Trade and Investment Partnership has long been the Atlanticists' last best hope. These countries—broadly those that joined the European Union since 2004—are for the most part instinctively pro-American, for reasons dating back to the Cold War. They see American engagement in Europe as the best bulwark against Russia. They are also instinctively free-market. They worry about the dirigiste, protectionist approach of some south European countries. They want an outward-looking, free-trading Europe that is open to new ideas, new markets—and new members, not a cozy club of stagnant and declining economies.

They have a third worry too: American disengagement from Europe. As memories of the titanic struggles against Nazism and Communism fade, they worry that the United States will look coolly and pragmatically at its relationship with Europe, and decide that other things—notably Asia—simply matter more. Even before the Obama administration's unwisely characterized "pivot to Asia" they sensed that the commitment to Europe was slipping. Since then they have begun to fear that it is irreversible and perhaps even unstoppable.

When TTIP was first broached, it therefore seemed like an answer to the eastern Europeans' prayers. The benefits were huge. For a start, even in narrow economic terms it was a good deal. East European consumers (who have much lower wages than their counterparts in the richer half of the continent) care chiefly about low prices. If American imports were able to enter the European market freely, the cash-strapped households of the eastern half of the continent would among the strongest beneficiaries.

More importantly on the import side, American hydro-carbon exports are a vital part of any European move away from the continent's over-dependence on Russian gas and oil. For now, America does not export crude oil and it will export Liquefied Natural Gas (LNG) only to countries with which it has a free trade agreement. It also lacks the physical infrastructure to sent LNG overseas in any significant quantities. LNG terminals will come into service from early 2016. Critics note that LNG from the United States will never flow to Europe in large enough quantities to replace the 160 billion cubic meters (bcm) which the EU imports from Russia, via four main import pipelines (North Stream across the Baltic sea, Yamal through Belarus, and the Bratstvo/Soyuz and Trans-Balkan pipelines through Ukraine).

But that is to miss the point. Even small amounts of LNG can be important bargaining tools for countries which other otherwise dependent on Russia as a monopoly supplier. Lithuania, for example, has spent $330 million on an LNG import terminal (a vessel called the *Independence*, which will be delivered from South Korea by the end of the year). Even before a drop of gas from that terminal actually reached Lithuania, Gazprom, the Russian gas giant, offered a 20% discount (Lithuania had previously been forced to pay some of the highest natural gas tariffs in Europe).

TTIP will stimulate American LNG exports to Europe, which will help create a more liquid LNG market, reducing risk and volatility and encouraging other providers to enter the fray. This virtuous circle could be a game-changer in the politics and economics of European energy security.

On the export side, the gains are more modest. The industrial champions of the post-communist region are mostly not great exporters. They are companies such as CEZ, the Czech electricity giant, or KGHM, the Polish copper and metals producer. Fairly few companies in the region at any level have big ambitions in North America. Most are still finding their feet in the 500 million-strong European single market. Some of the strongest performers are in service industries such as software—Poland's Comarch is an example—where they are largely unhampered by trade barriers. The biggest gains would be for niche exporters—artisanal foods, specialty cosmetics, and the like. Such small and medium-sized enterprises are daunted by the regulatory barriers of selling in North America, but are eyeing the post-TTIP market eagerly.

But the big gains would come from the effect of stimulating inward investment. Greater investor protection, and growing confidence and familiarity, would put the region on the map for smaller American investors—typically those making their first overseas investment or acquisition—who at the moment feel may daunted by the EU's complexity. It is worth noting that east Europeans are poised to gain disproportionately from any extra foreign investment that TTIP would bring. Their labor costs are still low, land is relatively cheap, and the infrastructure has improved sharply since accession, thanks to the tens of billions of euros that the EU has poured into the region as catch-up subsidies (the so-called "structural funds").

Against that, the costs of TTIP seem minor: genetically-modified food is unpopular in Hungary. American Budweiser is seen as an interloper in the Czech Republic, home to the original brew (from the town of Budvar, formerly Budweis). But overall few incumbent industries in the region would lose. If your domestic industries have survived German competition, you are unlikely to worry too much about America.

But the economic benefits are only part of a broader picture. For security-conscious east Europeans, American military and security engagement in the region will be most dependable if its anchored by strong trade and investment interests. Put bluntly, if some of the largest companies in the United States have big investments in eastern Europe, they will be invaluable allies on other issues.

To illustrate this, try a thought experiment. Imagine that Ukraine over the past 20 years had been run by determined economic reformers, rather than a bunch of incompetent kleptocrats. Imagine that as a result, the country's eastern and southern regions were not desolate, ill-run, hardscrabble places, dependent on Russia, but economically thriving, and studded with major American investments.

That may seem a stretch, but were it not for endemic corruption and bad government, Ukraine would be a tempting destination for outside investors. ADM, for example might have leapt into grain production in the "black earth" region, home to some of the most fertile soil in the world. U.S. Steel might have snapped up the metallurgy plants. Peabody would have seen great potential in the coal mines. The missile and defense-electronics factories of the east would have been prize catches for Raytheon, while Lockheed Martin and Boeing would have seen the potential of Ukraine's aviation industry. GE would be making turbines in Ukraine, while Exxon and Chevron would be developing the off-shore oil and gas fields. American companies would have bought the ports at Odessa and Mariupol. Crimea would have Californian-run wineries, with its decrepit sanatoria taken over by Marriott, Holiday Inn, Hilton and other chains, creating a world-class tourism destination.

In such an environment, recent events, such as the Russian takeover of Crimea, and the Kremlin-backed insurgency in eastern and southern Ukraine, would be unimaginable. Not only would the population in the vulnerable regions be far better off, and less vulnerable to propaganda and subversion, but the "Ukraine lobby" in Washington would be formidable. Messing with the United States is a bad idea. Messing with corporate America intensifies the danger.

This is just one of the lessons of the past year in Ukraine, all of which are clearest to those closest to the action. The frontline states in what is shaping up to be a new cold war with Russia—particularly Poland, Estonia, Latvia and Lithuania—believe that European policy towards Ukraine has been ill-conceived. It was quite right to try to woo Ukraine with an offer of a 'Deep and Comprehensive Free Trade Agreement'—part of what the European Union called its 'Eastern Partnership.' But to do so without realizing that Russia would find this an existential threat was the product of naïveté bordering on lunacy.

Trade was only the notional heart of the row. The EU did not want Ukraine to break its trade ties with Russia. The Kremlin, however, wanted Ukraine to sign up to its own trade arrangement, the Eurasian Economic Union—something that would have precluded a deal with the EU. More fundamentally, the Kremlin could not accept that with the EU's free-trade agreement, Ukraine would also embark on a civilizational shift: the slow, painful and belated modernization of its public services, judiciary, energy industry and financial system, bringing the country inevitably towards the standards needed for eventual membership of the EU.

For Russia, the idea that its largest and closest neighbor should be a prosperous, successful, law-governed democracy is not a dream; it is a nightmare. A central feature of the story that the Kremlin propaganda machine tells to the Russian people is that Western-style reform is a sham and a failure. Russia's top-down 'managed democracy' is better. If Ukraine came even close to disproving that thesis, it would prompt Russians to ask if their country might not also be better run. What would that mean for the cabal of ex-spooks, cronies and thugs who make up the regime in Moscow?

So the real row about Ukraine was not about that country's future, but about Russia's. It was also about the West: how hard would the EU (NATO has a back seat here) be prepared to push its model in territories which the Kremlin regards as its front yard?

The answer proved to be: not much. Vladimir Putin's habit of stamping on Western toes stems from a closely observed analysis of where we think our vital interests are. His assumption was that ultimately the West did not care greatly about Ukraine's territorial integrity, and was not prepared to make real sacrifices to deter Russia or to reverse the takeover of Crimea.

At the time this is being written, that seems to be right. The West has not imposed serious sanctions on Russia. It is prepared to accept the division of Ukraine and the continuing Russian-backed insurgency in that country's eastern provinces. It talks a tough game on sanctions but it is not prepared to take steps that would seriously dissuade the Kremlin, such as cutting arms sales to Russia (France has a large contract to build two amphibious-warfare vessels) or cutting Russians access to the capital market and the financial system (from which the City of London earns rich returns).

The frontline states of eastern Europe do not want to be the next Crimea. They know that their poorest regions are vulnerable to subversion. They know that integration with the world economy brings not only prosperity but also strengthens friendships and alliances. TTIP is the best possible way to ensure that the Atlantic alliance is rebooted on the basis of shared economic interests, overlaying the existing military and security ties with their roots in World War Two and the Cold War.

The problem is that these countries are not longer representative of the broader region. While Europe's Atlanticists were focusing on the vagaries of Washington policy-making during the Obama administration, another trend was developing under their noses: a new neutralism exemplified by the attitude of the Czech, Slovak, Hungarian and Bulgarian governments to the crisis in Ukraine.

These countries do not see a threat from Russia. They do not want higher defense spending. They do not want sanctions. They do not like the way that NATO and the EU have been reacting to the crisis. In the Czech and Slovak cases, they even say that they do not want other NATO countries to put troops on their soil—making insulting comparisons with the Soviet-led invasion of the former Czechoslovakia in 1968. Among the "new neutralists," enthusiasm for TTIP is conspicuous by its absence. Hungary has even become a cheerleader for South Stream, a Russian-backed pipeline which is being promoted in defiance of EU warnings that it breaches the rules of the single market.

This is a huge and sudden shift. Time was when the countries of what Donald Rumsfeld called 'New Europe' formed a coherent entity. They were all keen on European institutions having a dominant role as the continent's rule-setters. That, they believed, was the best way of keeping the big countries of Europe, with their protectionist agendas and ingrained distaste to the east Europeans, in check. And they all worried about Russia. Even before the chauvinist, revisionist tendencies of Vladimir Putin disturbed the horizon in Brussels and Washington, DC, security-policy experts in Tallinn, Riga, Vilnius, Warsaw, Prague, Bratislava and elsewhere were profoundly concerned by what they saw in the eastern neighborhood.

As a result, though the basic plusses and minuses of TTIP remain unchanged, what is missing now, in much of the region, is the political momentum. Trade deals require a political jolt to overcome vested interests and bureaucratic lethargy. Even two or three years ago, TTIP would have found some of its strongest supporters in the eastern half of the continent, where political leaders saw the deal as not just an economic matter, but a geopolitical game-changer.

The battle for TTIP must now be waged without countries that could once be counted on as allies. In their place may come others. One is Ukraine. Although not part of the EU, it would benefit from

TTIP. The most hopeful moments in the past year have come when the United States and the EU have closely coordinated their policies in Ukraine—notably in pushing the former regime, of the now-disgraced ex-president Viktor Yanukovych, to bite the bullet and accept the painful reforms that the EU association agreement required. Similarly, the most disastrous occasions have come when the EU and the United States seemed to be letting their policies drift apart. Ukraine will benefit from a broader and deeper market in LNG—meaning that it can import gas, if necessary, from Europe rather than being dependent on Russian supplies.

The other new allies are Sweden and Finland—two countries that are not members of NATO, but which are deeply concerned by the insecurity of the northeast European region. It would be nice to think that these countries—both free traders with strong export industries—would step up to fill the gap left by the central and southeastern Europeans. But there is not much sign of it. The Atlanticist center-right Swedish government is heading for defeat in parliamentary elections in 2014. Finland's shaky coalition government appears unwilling to take tough decisions on national security. More menacing behavior from the Kremlin may concentrate minds in Stockholm and Helsinki. But these are flimsy hopes, compared with those that rested on eastern Europe in its Atlanticist heyday.

The big winner from the clouds that hang over TTIP is clear: Russia. Even during the Soviet era, the Kremlin was determined to sever the bond between Europe and the United States. It pumped money and political support into neutralist and anti-American forces, notably the anti-Vietnam campaigns of the 1960s and 1970s, and the ecological and the anti-nuclear movements of the 1980s. That was a hard sell. Europeans were more scared of the Soviet Union than they were disdainful of America.

Since the collapse of communism, that has become easier. Many Europeans see no reason to feel grateful to America, and no reason to feel scared of Russia—a diminished force which no longer preaches a messianic, totalitarian ideology. Under Vladimir Putin, Russia has seized its opportunity created by American missteps and European complacency. It has used business and financial links (especially in the energy sector) to build murky mutually beneficial ties with European politicians. It misses no chance to sow dissension between the United States and its European allies, on issues ranging from the Iraq war to issues of internet freedom and digital privacy. The furor surrounding the fugitive NSA contractor Edward Snowden exemplifies this. Germans routinely tell opinion pollsters that they see America as a greater threat to world peace than Russia. Moscow puts money into think-tanks and universities to promote anti-Americanism, and publishes well-financed supplements in cash-strapped media publications (such as Britain's *Daily Telegraph*). The RT television channel (formerly known as Russia Today) has become a source of anti-American propaganda which matches the most venomous Soviet broadcasters at the height of the Cold War—and enjoys a far greater reach.

TTIP presents a huge challenge to the Russian plan to divide Europe from the United States. It offers something that the Kremlin cannot match: a transparent, mutually beneficial agreement which creates a rules-based framework for international cooperation.

By contrast, the Kremlin's struggling rival project, the Eurasian Economic Union, is a secretive and discretionary affair, in which all economic and commercial considerations are subordinate to political considerations. The Eurasian Union is indeed in trouble. Other countries in Russia's shadow, such as Kazakhstan and Belarus, are deeply unhappy with the Kremlin's neo-imperialist approach, even if they also recognize that they have no immediate alternative but to go along with it.

If TTIP succeeds, it will change the political and economic landscape of Eurasia for decades. There will be no more doubt about American commitment to Europe. Eastern Europe's economic security will be particularly enhanced, both through stronger economic growth (and the social cohesion that goes with it) but also through stronger energy ties. The eastern hinterland (Ukraine, Moldova and Belarus) will benefit too. The magnetic attraction to the West will grow. Russia's economic model, based on the collection and distribution of natural-resource and bureaucratic rents, will look even more out of date and unattractive. It is hardly surprising that the Kremlin is making such efforts to derail TTIP. It is rather more surprising that we are so averse to noticing them.

Chapter 6

TTIP's Implications for the Global Economic Integration of Central and Eastern Europe

Tamás Novák

Impact analyses and empirical results of existing studies on the economic impacts of the Transatlantic Trade and Investment Partnership (TTIP) show significant benefits for the participating countries. Eleven out of the 28 members of the European Union (EU) are from central Europe ("new" member states) and they are mostly small countries with open economies. The impact on less developed member states of the central European region can be even greater. It can contribute to their deeper integration into the global economic networks through investments, but their underdevelopment rightly calls for caution. The implications and the direction of potential policy responses are less clear in the rest of eastern Europe. According to some studies, third countries would be facing losses, and little has been said about the potential impacts on eastern Europe. Russia, one of the largest emerging countries, has formulated very ambitious foreign economic and policy objectives. It is trying to restore its economic and political sphere of influence. Russia and other countries from the region might forcefully respond to possible trade diversion effects and worsening competitiveness if the agreement contains significant changes.

Central and eastern Europe (CEE) has started integrating into the global markets only recently after the breakup of planned economic systems. This region has been compared to Latin American countries in the early 1970s in terms of its international economic integration pattern. Latin America and eastern Europe shared important macroeconomic characteristics in the final third of the twentieth century. In this period, both regions displayed similar economic performances, although their economic and political systems were vastly different. A common feature of the two regions was that they were at the periphery of the international economy and were facing comparable structural challenges while international economic developments exerted identical external pressures on them. Economic growth slowed, the terms of trade deteriorated, trade balances worsened. This led to dynamically increasing foreign debt, and its servicing consumed large parts of export revenues. Rising indebtedness did not serve to speed up structural change.[1] In both regions the 1990s brought about significant transformation, deep economic changes, and renewed efforts to achieve quicker economic growth. On average, Latin America and eastern Europe went through significant transformation, Russia and Brazil and other countries have been considered as rapidly growing large emerging markets. At the same time, regional integration efforts as well as WTO membership became important drivers of international economic integration for several countries in both regions. Despite the remarkable growth performance in international comparison and the major advances in catching up with developed countries, their peripheral/semi-peripheral position has not changed significantly. In many respects, they are facing the same challenges of globalization, regional integration, closing the gap and economic sovereignty.

After the collapse of the planned economic system, most advanced central European countries managed to adopt the key institutions of a market economy and liberal democracy. The European Union has become the most important trading partner for all of them, but policy orientations, economic growth and democratic transformation showed big differences across the region. Today, there are two fundamentally different and distinct country groups in eastern Europe. The first group consists of countries that have either become members of the European Union, or were intending to enter the EU and are already negotiating membership. Some other countries in this group have association agreements with the EU.[2] These countries have chosen the path of global integration through integration into a large single market by giving up several instruments of their external economic policy. The other group mostly comprises countries that do not possess a

---

[1]Ivan T. Berend, "End of Century. Global Transition to a Market Economy: Laissez-Faire on the Peripheries?" in Ivan T. Berend, ed., *Transition to a Market Economy at the End of the 20th Century* (Munich: Südosteuropa-Gesellschaft, 2004).

[2]In the region, negotiations are currently underway with Serbia and Montenegro. Candidate or potential candidate countries are the Former Yugoslav Republic of Macedonia, Albania, Bosnia and Herzegovina, and Kosovo.

realistic perspective of EU membership, or nations that do not intend to join at all.[3]

EU member states from central Europe may be viewed as a broadly coherent group that shares similar interests, although their economic and political strategies may vary from time to time. Russia, after more than a decade-long decline, is the largest emerging economic and political power in eastern Europe today, and has a clear intention to shape the future of the region. This country is gaining more and more importance in the Eurasian space and pursues a dissimilar strategy to what is followed by EU member states. In recent years Russia has initiated an ambitious integration project with the final objective of creating a Eurasian Economic Union.[4] In addition, it has also sought to expand its influence westwards by using its natural resources and capital investments.

Impact of the TTIP and Economic Theories

The advantages of a TTIP agreement are supposed to be similar to those that were forecast before the creation of the European Single Market. The internal market in a simple form is based on the neoclassical approach: eliminating trade and investment barriers equals increasing trade and investment activity because of bigger expected returns, efficient labor market, etc. These advantages are supposed to come from eliminating the distortions of competition. In theory, consumers in each country gain from lower prices and any losses to the local producers will be more than compensated by the gains from greater competition. Increased competition and enlarged market opportunities stimulate the development and use of new technologies that improve productivity, decrease costs, increase living standards,

---

[3]Tamás Novák, "Changes in Ukraine and the Future of Central and Eastern Europe," Center for Transatlantic Relations, 2014. accessed at: http://transatlantic.sais-jhu.edu/publications/NovakT-Changes%20in%20the%20Ukraine.pdf. The European Union has its Eastern Partnership (EAP) policy aimed at creating deep free trade with post-Soviet states: Armenia, Azerbaijan, Belarus, Georgia, Moldova, Ukraine.

[4]The EurAsEC Customs Union became increasingly important for Russia since the launch of EAP. Its members: Russia, Kazakhstan, Belarus. Armenia and Kyrgyzstan are expected to join the Union soon.

etc. By doing so economic growth rates will be higher and new jobs will be created.[5]

This strong belief in market forces and the positive-sum game of liberalization for each participant seems to be a bit strange at first sight, so soon after an economic crisis when more cautious strands of economic thinking are on the rise. The benefits of market forces and external liberalization have been questioned, weakening the unconditional mainstream belief in their beneficial effects.[6] As far as the benefits of single-market-type integration are concerned, we may argue from the opposite perspective as well in terms of costs: the single market idea involves channeling the negative implications of globalization, including (1) loss of jobs, because of increased competition; (2) disappearing industries because of weaker, smaller domestic economic actors; (3) negative impact on structurally weak regions. This last impact was expected to be eased by regional and structural policies, though these are seemingly without success as reflected in intensifying regional differences within the EU.

The objective of the EU Single Market was to deliver higher growth rates to keep up the pace and successfully compete with fast-growing emerging regions. Its impacts are not entirely about success and assessments are only superficially addressing these problems.[7] Even if there are arguments to support that the current problems of the EU have not all been caused by the operation of the Single Market, several politicians and the public perceive the Single Market as a failure.[8] During the past two decades, in relative terms, in comparison

---

[5]Stefan Vetter, *The Single European Market. 20 Years on Achievements, Unfulfilled Expectations & Further Potential* (Frankfurt am Main: Deutsche Bank AG, DB Research, 2013), p. 4.

[6]As Joseph Stiglitz writes, "Neo-liberal market fundamentalism was always a political doctrine serving certain interests. It was never supported by economic theory. Nor, it should now be clear, is it supported by historical experience. Learning this lesson may be the silver lining in the cloud now hanging over the global economy," accessed at: http://www.project-syndicate.org/commentary/the-end-of-neo-liberalism-

[7]Bas Straathof, Gert-Jan Linders, Arjan Lejour and Jan Möhlmann, *The Internal Market and the Dutch Economy: Implications for Trade and Economic Growth* (CPB Netherlands Bureau for Economic Policy Analysis, 2008); Copenhagen Economics, *Delivering a Stronger Single Market* (Nordic Innovation Publication 2012, p. 11); Andrea Boltho and Barry Eichengreen, *The Economic Impact of European Integration*, CEPR Discussion Paper 6820, 2008.

[8]According to Commission calculations, between 1992 and 2008 an additional 2.13% GDP growth and 2.77 million jobs were created. See European Commission, Communication

with the rest of the world, the EU's economic performance has deteriorated, which may suggest that the primary objective of the Single Market has not been fulfilled. It is clear that all of the *ex-ante* assessments were unrealistically optimistic about the positive impacts of the Single Market[9] and were unable to properly address the negative impacts the less developed members would face.

Impact assessments to date generally show that each country participating in the TTIP gets benefits; the only question left to answer is the extent of such benefits, as they may vary from country to country and be largely a function of the content of the agreement.[10] If problem areas (agriculture, culture, etc.) were taken out of the deal, most of the benefits could not be felt and the advantages would be significantly lower.[11] Disregarding the fact that none of the impact assessments is capable of grasping the implications entirely, and even less able to calculate with unexpected political and economic changes, not to mention unpredictability of the reactions of third countries, the case of the EU internal market—and experiences of other FTAs (Free Trade Agreements)—prove that less developed countries may lose with liberalization and the

---

from the Commission to the European Parliament, the Council, the European Economic and Social Committee and the Committee of the Regions, Brussels, 3.10.2012. com(2012) 573 final, 2012. It would be interesting to see how many more jobs and how much more GDP was lost because of the deep integration among the countries. "The Single Market (...) is less popular than ever, while Europe needs it more than ever.... The Single Market is seen as 'yesterday's business' compared to other policy priorities." Mario Monti, *A New Strategy for the Single Market at the Service of Europe's Economy and Society.* Report to the President of the European Commission, 2010, http://ec.europa.eu/internal_market/strategy/docs/ monti_report_final_10_05_2010_en.pdf, p. 6.

[9]The Cecchini Report calculated a potential wealth effect of 4.25-6.5% of GDP for the twelve member states in the Single Market. None of the ex-post assessments proves more than 2 percent, and "... an economic assessment of the Single Market ... brings with it the conceptual difficulty of separating the impact of the Single Market not only from the consequences of globalization, but also from the introduction of the euro." Vetter, op. cit, p. 3.; Cecchini, Paolo & Catinat, Michel & Jacquemin, Alexis. 1988. *The European Challenge 1992: The Benefits of a Single Market.* Aldershot: Wildwood House Limited.

[10]Centre for Economic Policy Research (CEPR), *Reducing Transatlantic Barriers to Trade and Investment. An Economic Assessment.* Final Project Report, March 2013; Gabriel Felbermayr, Benedikt Heid and Sybille Lehwald, *Transatlantic Trade and Investment Partnership (TTIP). Who Benefits from a Free Trade Deal?* (Gütersloh: Bertelsmann Stiftung, 2013); Gabriel J. Felbermayr and Mario Larch, "The Transatlantic Trade and Investment Partnership (TTIP): Potentials, Problems and Perspectives," *CESifo Forum* 2/2013 (June).

[11]CEPR, *op. cit.,* p. 2.

opening up of markets. The case of Greece and other southern countries of the EU clearly prove that problems with FTAs and other integration initiatives can be numerous. Less developed countries of the European Union, or those that are not competitive enough, would not gain as much as is forecasted; what is more, the risk of losing is not negligible, especially if inappropriate economic policies are pursued. The prospect of gaining less or even sustaining losses by underdeveloped countries is in line with economic theories that do not believe in positive sum impacts of international economic liberalization.[12]

EU Members from Central and Eastern Europe

The potential benefits of small, open economies that deeply integrated into the international division of labor, such as the "new EU members" that joined the EU in 2004, 2007, and 2013, are believed to be significant. Some of them have export openness indicators above the 75-80% range (export/GDP) and their import activities are also significant because of the high import intensity of their export production. This integration into the international division of labor and openness to trade explains why the calculations on the effects of TTIP indicate above average benefits for them. Apparently, they are interested in liberalization and trade facilitation that helps to further expand their exports. Increasing foreign sales are essentially important for their sustainable growth. Because of the small domestic market and the limited local purchasing power, if firms in these countries aim at increasing sales and creating more jobs, they simply have no alternatives to internationalization. Their exports are mostly based on the

---

[12]This strategy proved successful for example in the United States and Germany (when they were less developed than their trading partners), and much later in some of the emerging Far East regions. "In the first stage they must adopt free trade with the more advanced nations as a means of raising themselves from a state of barbarism and of making advances in agriculture. In the second stage they must resort to commercial restrictions to promote the growth of manufactures, fisheries, navigation, and foreign trade. In the last stage, after reaching the highest degree of wealth and power, they must gradually revert to the principle of free trade and of unrestricted competition in the home as well as in foreign markets, so that their agriculturists, manufacturers, and merchants may be preserved from indolence and stimulated to retain the supremacy which they have acquired." Friedrich List, *The National System of Political Economy by Friedrich List*. Trans. Sampson S. Lloyd, with an Introduction by J. Shield Nicholson (London: Longmans, Green and Co., 1916) p. xx.

performance of FDI-related manufacturing and services firms, and they need to elaborate strategies that preserve and strengthen export orientation. (This should not mean the negligence of domestic demand factors—consumption and investment—but their primary role is to balance the growth pattern, rather than replace export orientation with domestic demand driven strategy, at least at the current level of economic development). The success of export-led growth strategy depends on several factors and there are a number of risks and challenges of such a strategy as well.[13] But countries that implement strategies that disregard export orientation will soon face sustainability problems.

Because central European countries cannot compete with really low-wage countries from the Far East (though their wages are still low in international comparison), long-term sustainable strategies cannot avoid upgrading technological capabilities by attracting more FDI. If the conditions of doing business are improved, the rule of law is upheld, productivity is increased, they could count on increasing investment from U.S. firms already before the TTIP enters into force.[14] Increased FDI from U.S. production and services firms is the most important source of possible benefit of the TTIP in the central European member states. The realistic and sustainable economic strategy of these countries should focus on the further modernization of their export structure and the upgrading of technology. This, however, would require large investments in human and physical infrastructure and the improvement of the business environment. If these conditions are fulfilled, theoretically, TTIP would again open a window of opportunity for several countries to utilize the agreement for the purpose of accelerating economic growth.

An additional benefit may be related to investments made by third countries. Participation in integration initiatives influences transaction costs for third countries that raise the question of production within

---

[13] Andras Inotai, "Sustainable Growth Based on Export-oriented Economic Strategy," *Economic Policy Analyses*, FES-EPI, 2013, p. 5, accessed at: http://library.fes.de/pdf-files/bueros/sofia/10070.pdf.

[14] Daniel Hamilton, "The Changing Nature of the Transatlantic Link: U.S. Approaches and Implications for Central and Eastern Europe," *Communist and Post-Communist Studies* 46, 2013, p. 308.

the integration area or export there. Integration initiatives (even in their simplest form, i.e. free trade area) are creating incentives for third countries to invest within integrated areas in order to avoid trade-related costs. Theoretically, they can encourage firms—that may eventually want to export to the United States—to invest in central Europe.[15] An investment boom of this kind was evident prior to the EU accession of the central European countries. The impact of FDI was largely tangible before the accession took place, not least because of the extra-EU investments.[16] The volume of such investments would not be too large, but it is potentially to be reckoned with.

On the other hand, however, the risk of smaller than expected impacts is high, which makes the picture for "new members" and other peripheral EU countries a little more obscure.[17] The problem is that in several countries the economy has a dual structure; a few large transnational firms are integrated into the international production chains, while the rest of the economy is unable to participate in international trade, because it lacks exportable, competitive products. In addition, not least because of the internal problems of the European Union and the increasing Russian influence in the region, the regional political commitment to liberal economic order and democracy is not at all guaranteed. And this is an increasingly serious issue in a region where economic and political transformation was thought to firmly integrate countries into the system of Western institutions and values. The changes in political and economic policy strategies may increase business risks in certain countries.

Taking all factors taken into consideration, the benefits for the less developed central European countries in terms of export, FDI and GDP growth is probably larger than the disadvantages.[18] It is explained

---

[15]Daniel S. Hamilton and Joseph P. Quinlan, *The Transatlantic Economy 2013. Annual Survey of Jobs, Trade and Investment between the United States and Europe* (Washington, DC: Center for Transatlantic Relations, Johns Hopkins University, Paul H. Nitze School of Advanced International Studies, 2013), p. vi.

[16]Alan A. Bevan and Saul Estrin, "The Determinants of Foreign Direct Investment into European Transition Economies," *Journal of Comparative Economics* 32, 2004, p. 777.

[17]Central and Eastern Europe Development Institute (CEED), *The Transatlantic Trade and Investment Agreement (TTIP)—Key Issues and Challenges Ahead,* Bulletin of Central and Eastern Europe No. 4, 2013, p. 5.

[18]Center for European Policy Analysis (CEPA), "TTIP: What Will It Do for Central Europe?" Central Europe Digest, August 6, 2013, p. 6.

by their pattern of division of labor that is based on export orientation of foreign-owned firms. All these favorable impacts, however, can be utilized only if the business environment is favorable enough. There is, however a substantial risk that policies in the region may become inward-looking and more protectionist. This risk is strengthened by the weak performance of the European economy and the unfulfilled expectations of the EU membership in terms of catching up.

The choice of economic and political models of Central European governments may be influenced by the economic performance of advanced and emerging countries. There is a danger that regional governments and politicians see the EU as a weak economic center whose economic and political model is inadequate to respond to current and future global challenges. The increasing skepticism may lead to the conclusion that, instead of the European model, they should follow potentially more successful strategies. Anti-EU economic and political strategies in the countries shattered by economic difficulties, characterized by relatively poor economic outlook, and declining standards of living, however, are on the increase. Developments over the past few years could easily lead to the introduction of measures that are shockingly different from European traditions and that would probably weaken the ties that have developed over the past more than two decades. Economic integration can be considered "too deep" because the original objective of economic and political transformation has not been achieved[19] and, instead of convergence on the living standards of more developed countries, a more complicated balance has been experienced. The situation could easily worsen. Tempted by the almost unlimited power of leaders in some post-Soviet countries, democratic systems could morph into something "new," into very destructive, obsolete structures in which country identity is defined in opposition to the European development model. If that happens, the possible favorable implications of TTIP will not be felt in the affected countries.

Russia

The original idea that the TTIP agreement can be beneficial for each country in the long run relies on the presumption that "the eco-

---

[19]The argument of too deep integration is not only a way of thinking of central Europe, but similar dilemmas are worded in more developed EU members too.

nomic importance of the EU and the United States will mean that their partners will also have an incentive to move towards the new transatlantic standards."[20] In other words, third countries would face such immense losses that it would be their very interest to join the TTIP. This is an overly optimistic forecast of the prospective developments. Turning to the third countries in central and eastern Europe, the key question is Russia, which would definitely take the TTIP for what it really means for this country—a geopolitical aspiration that may threaten Russia's position in Europe. The important political objective behind the TTIP is that this large-scale bilateral agreement increases the incentives of third parties to achieve further liberalization steps at the multilateral level. This way the TTIP (the advanced countries) becomes a rule setter in international trade for third countries. It would lead the EU and the United States to regain a leading position in international trade and economic development. This expectation is realistic only if third countries feel that it is in their interest to accept the rules elaborated by developed economies. This situation would be similar to the decades preceding the economic rise of large emerging countries, when developing or less developed countries were not able to defend their interests against the advanced countries in international economic organizations. This is also the fundamental issue concerning countries such as China, Russia, India, and Brazil or other large emerging markets.

None of the scenarios in the existing analyses calculate openly with potential countermeasures taken by third countries. A more realistic approach is to examine three scenarios: (1) large emerging countries may think that they will not lose too much if the agreement finally remains limited in scope; (2) the TTIP may be a strong incentive for new agreements and instruments within the framework of WTO negotiations with the objective of reducing the negative implications; (3) third countries will increasingly look for countermeasures. The first two alternatives are clearly far more beneficial for the advanced world. Regarding the third choice, this would result in the intensification of creating trade blocs (that may lead to the increasing disruption of global trade) and/or instruments which make export and invest-

---

[20]European Commission, 2013. Member States Endorse EU-US Trade and Investment Negotiations. European Commission—MEMO/13/564, accessed at: http://europa.eu/rapid/press-release_MEMO-13-564_en.htm.

ment from advanced countries more difficult. In addition, more concerted efforts and countermeasures from large emerging countries cannot be ruled out if international economic relations are aggravated. Closer cooperation between large emerging countries regarding international trade would suffice to establish a common ground for asserting similar interests. Should that come about, it will probably disrupt global trade and the current institutional system.

Russia has been able to strengthen its position in international relations and become strong enough to try to regain and increase its influence in some parts of the CIS (Commonwealth of Independent States). Russia's efforts to reintegrate a part of the CIS will continue and strengthen as a number one priority in its foreign policy. Regarding economic issues, Russia is becoming an increasingly important player in the eastern part of Europe and in Asia.[21] In recent years, the country has become one of the most important capital investors in the world, mostly through state-owned enterprises, though obviously not independently from politics, and it has become the number one investor in the east European region.[22] In coming years it is most likely to strengthen further its efforts to be involved in European business. In addition to achieving economic penetration, it is also more and more in Moscow's interest to stop the spread of Western-style democracy, perhaps even in countries where it seemed to be solidly rooted.[23]

In addition to geopolitical considerations, the most important issue for Russia relates to the energy sector. If TTIP eases access to U.S. gas, it will benefit both European consumers and the industry. (On the other hand, cheap gas exports to Europe would erode the competitive advantage of U.S. firms over European competitors.) At the same time, this new source of natural gas would substantially diminish

---

[21]Ilan Berman, *Implosion: The End of Russia and What It Means for America*. New York: Regnery Publishing, 2013.

[22]United Nations Conference on Trade and Development (UNCTAD), *World Investment Report*. New York: United Nations, 2013, pp. 8, 13.

[23]See for example the citation from an interview with Francis Fukuyama: "I think that's right, that Russia doesn't have an interest in having a healthy democracy on its borders because that's going to give the wrong signals to its own people. So I think it's probably right that Russia would prefer to have other authoritarian neighbors around it." Francis Fukuyama, 2013. Democratization in Eastern Europe. RFE/RL, accessed at: http://www.rferl.org/content/interview-fukuyama-democratization-eastern-europe/25087539.html.

Table 1. Geographical Pattern of Russian Merchandise Trade

(% of total export or import)

Export	2005	2012	Import	2005	2012
Total	100.00	100.00	Total	100.00	100.00
EU	53.63	48.96	EU	42.79	40.34
Germany	8.17	6.79	Germany	13.45	12.11
Netherlands	10.19	14.63	Italy	4.47	4.24
Italy	7.89	6.18	France	3.72	4.36
CEE6*	10.59	8.41	CEE6*	5.91	6.98
CIS	13.51	14.94	CIS	19.24	13.77
China	5.40	6.81	China	7.36	16.39
USA	2.62	2.47	USA	4.62	4.85
Rest of the World	24.84	26.82	Rest of the World	25.99	24.65

Source: Own calculation, Central Bank of Russia.
*Bulgaria, Czech Republic, Hungary, Poland, Slovakia, Romania.

Europe's dependence on Russian gas, which is disadvantageous to Russia from macroeconomic and geopolitical perspectives. As European demand decreases, Russia will be increasingly forced to reorient its energy exports to other markets, and gain influence mostly through investments in the European energy and financial sectors. There are clear signs that Russia seeks exert influence over as many European assets as possible. The biggest opportunity for Russia to do that is in the central European region with which it can partly substitute its losses in natural gas exports provided that U.S. gas is imported more easily. In addition, Russia can restrict its imports from Europe in response, since Moscow uses trade policy as a political tool, despite its recent WTO membership. If Russia considers that its loss is too big in Europe and it is not possible to regain a share of it in other parts of the globe, then it can use its imports from Europe as a bargaining power.

To sum up, energy is a sensitive issue for the Russian economy and the danger of worsening Russian positions in the European market may cause Russia to control as many countries as it is possible through oil, gas, nuclear power generation or financial sector investments. The TTIP could be an important element in the changes of the global energy landscape. After the conclusion of the TTIP, sooner or later U.S. natural gas exports will definitely and significantly increase. It

Table 2. Russia's Trade with the EU by SITC section 2012

(% of total export or import)

		Export	Import
0	Food and live animals	0.6	6.7
1	Beverages and tobacco	0.0	1.3
2	Crude materials, inedible, except fuels	0.9	1.4
3	Mineral fuels, lubricants and related materials	76.3	1.1
4	Animal and vegetable oils, fats and waxes	0.2	0.4
5	Chemicals and related products, n.e.c	3.0	15.8
6	Manufactured goods classified chiefly by material	6.4	10.3
7	Machinery and transport equipment	0.9	49.6
8	Miscellaneous manufactured articles	0.2	11.9
9	Commodities and transactions n.e.c	2.8	0.8

Source: European Commission, Directorate-General for Trade.

could have serious geopolitical implications for Europe's own relationship with Russia.

Conclusion

The impact of the TTIP on central and eastern Europe depends on the details of the final agreement. There are three scenarios; each has very different implications both for members and third countries.

(1) Since the aim of the TTIP is political, the discussion will concentrate on regulations and standards (trade, consumer safety, environment, etc.), but because of the conflicts between the EU and the United States concerning the underlying principles, without achieving sizeable results.

(2) The TTIP breaks away from prevailing international trade patterns because it leads to new standards that are protectionist against third countries such as China, India, Russia, etc. Global trade becomes fragmented with intensifying role of regional blocs.

(3) The third alternative is an open TTIP that encourages third countries to join. As a result, the TTIP would become the core of a new global trading system where the rule setters are once again the most advanced economies.

It is impossible to see today which of these alternatives will become a reality. If TTIP develops into a deep, comprehensive agreement, its impact will be far greater. In this case central European member countries of the EU would theoretically gain a lot due to their integration into the division of labor, mostly through transnational firms at different levels of their supplier chain. If the governments of these countries pursue outward-looking economic policies and improve their business environment, this would attract additional foreign direct investments, mostly from U.S. firms, but an increase in investment from third countries can also not be ruled out entirely. However, the risk of inward-looking policies in this region is intensifying, which would render the utilization of opportunities even more difficult.

Regarding third countries from the region, the strategy Russia chooses to adopt seems to be the most important. The negative implications of a deep TTIP would be intense. The first impact would be related to trade diversion in the short run. The long term implication is, however, much more serious and relates to Russian energy exports that make up around 75% of Russian sales to the EU. As the TTIP would improve the market access of U.S. energy to Europe, Russian energy exports would be seriously hit. To counterbalance these negative implications, in addition to export reorientation towards other countries, Moscow may seek to increase its influence in other sectors through investments into European assets. In an extreme case, the TTIP may trigger stronger cooperation among large emerging countries to formulate concerted efforts to neutralize negative consequences of the agreement.

Chapter 7

TTIP and Turkey:
The Geopolitical Dimension

Kemal Kirişci

The launch of the Transatlantic Trade and Investment Partnership (TTIP) negotiations in the summer of 2013 has attracted considerable attention. This attention has been primarily focused on the economic dimension of TTIP, often at the expense of geopolitical considerations. This is not surprising, because TTIP aspires to create a much more deeply integrated transatlantic market composed of 28 European Union (EU) member countries and the United States. This market would cater to a population close to one billion people commanding 47% of the world's GDP and close to 27% of world trade.[1] TTIP negotiations aim to achieve much more than traditional trade liberalization by lowering or removing remaining already low level barriers to trade. They aspire to address tougher non-tariff barriers (NTBs) by harmonizing regulatory issues and move on to a WTO-plus agenda to govern reciprocal investments and open up new sectors such as agriculture, government procurements and services to international competition. The immediate objectives of TTIP have frequently been defined as boosting the sluggish EU and U.S. economies by providing for economic growth and employment through increased trade and an expansion of reciprocal foreign direct investments. Domestic political considerations have led EU and U.S. politicians, not surprisingly, to emphasize these economic objectives.

However, TTIP, especially with its sister Trans-Pacific Partnership (TPP), also offers a number of geopolitical objectives. The spirit behind these objectives has been captured succinctly by Stuart Eizenstat, former U.S. Deputy Secretary of the Treasury and U.S. Ambassador to the EU, who noted that

---

[1]Calculated from *IMF International Financial Statistics*, April 2014, http://elibrary-data.imf.org/ and *IMF World Economic Outlook*, April 2014, http://www.imf.org/external/pubs/ft/weo/2014/01/weodata/index.aspx. If the trade within the EU is also taken into consideration the figure of 27% would increase by another 15-42% percent of world trade.

> There are essentially two competing models of governance in the post-Communist world. One is the transatlantic model shared by many other countries, based upon democratic governance, with free peoples, free markets, and free trade; the other is autocratic governance, state-controlled or dominated economies, and managed trade. The TTIP is an opportunity to show the world that our model of governance can produce tangible gains for our people on both sides of the Atlantic and more broadly are the best model to meet the challenges of the 21st century.[2]

Recently, the contest between these two forms of governance has become particularly visible with respect to events that have unfolded in Ukraine since November 2013. Street protests broke out against the then President of Ukraine, Viktor Yanukovych, for having backed down from initialing an association agreement with the EU in preference for deeper economic relations with Russia and the prospects of Ukraine entering the Russian led Eurasian customs union. The protests culminated in Yanukovych fleeing the country and a caretaker government being formed to prepare the country for national elections. However, in the meantime Russian President Vladimir Putin's reluctance to "lose" Ukraine led to a series of events that in March 2014 saw the Russian annexation of Crimea and since then efforts to undermine Ukraine's territorial integrity. Armenia, on the other hand, was unable to resist Russian pressures when it was forced to suspend negotiations with the EU and join the customs union with Russia. For the time being Georgia and Moldava have avoided a similar fate and have taken important steps towards greater integration with the EU. They signed their association agreements with the EU in June 2014.

What has unfolded in Ukraine can be seen as a geopolitical contest that erupted over different models of economic integration and forms of governance. Many recognize that if Ukraine's relations with the EU can be deepened this would matter significantly in terms of the geopolitical interests of the transatlantic community. In the words of Ambassador Paula Dobriansky, former U.S. Undersecretary of State

---

[2]Stuart E. Eizenstat, "Transatlantic Trade and Investment Partnership (TTIP) Remarks," Woodrow Wilson International Center for Scholars, (Washington, DC: March 21, 2013), http://www.acus.org/files/transcripts/seizenstat130321wilsonremarks.pdf.

for Democracy and Global Affairs, whichever way Ukraine goes matters significantly for the whole region surrounding Ukraine.[3]

Another region that is a source of geopolitical contestation is the Middle East. When the Arab Spring first erupted in December 2010, there were heightened expectations that the Arab world might finally be transformed in the direction of greater democracy, rule of law and liberal market economies. With the possible exception of Tunisia, this still has not happened. Instead—except for oil-producing Gulf countries—the Arab world is in the throes of deep economic and political instability. Egypt, as the traditional leader of the Arab world, remains in a state of turmoil where a regime reminiscent of the one preceding the Arab Spring appears to be emerging. Worst of course is the case of Iraq and Syria. The future of both countries as unified entities is in question. The influence of the EU and the United States over the future course of these countries is extremely limited, and is further blocked and contested by Russia and Iran. In the case of Syria, Russia clearly supports the existing Assad regime. Iran also backs the Syrian regime as well as the one in Baghdad that continues to advance repressive and polarizing policies that aggravate instability in Iraq. It will clearly be a long time before the Arab world reaches a modicum of stability so that the thought of easing this world into a transatlantic form of governance can even be entertained. Currently, the geopolitical contest over these two countries is far from favoring the interests of the EU and the United States.

Turkey is a country that sits in the midst of these two highly contested regions. Turkey has been a long-standing ally of the United States and a member of the transatlantic alliance. However, lately it has been having domestic political problems and questions have been raised about Turkey's commitment to transatlantic values. Questions have also been raised about Turkey's foreign policy.[4] Nevertheless, Turkey has been a loyal member of NATO since 1952 and was a founding member of many of the Western-led economic and political organizations ranging from GATT, the IMF and World Bank to the

---

[3] Remarks made at the "Three Ambassadors to Discuss Ukraine's Turn to Russia, Impact on U.S. and E.U.," the Bipartisan Policy Center, Washington DC, January 14, 2014.

[4] *Back to Zero Problems? Recent Developments in Turkey's Foreign Policy*, (Washington DC: Bipartisan Policy Center, April 2014).

OECD and the Council of Europe. Turkey has had an association agreement with the European Economic Community since 1963 and a customs union with the EU in place since 1996. Furthermore, even if sporadically, Turkey is moving forward in negotiations regarding its membership to the EU since 2005.

Despite a foreign policy that is at times assertive and independently minded, Turkey's economic and social ties with its traditional transatlantic allies remain very strong. In 2013 44% of Turkey's foreign trade was with the EU and the United States; more than two-thirds of foreign direct investment in Turkey came from the EU and the U.S. while 66% of Turkish capital was invested there.[5] In the course of the last decade, the Turkish economy has grown impressively and has become the seventh largest economy in Europe (including Russia), and the 17th largest in the world. In 2013, the economy of Turkey was larger than those of all its neighbors put together, excluding Iran and Russia, demonstrating its importance for the economies of the region. Furthermore, this economic performance precipitated the emergence of a vibrant middle class, which now plays a critical role in Turkey's democracy. An overwhelming majority of this middle class travels to EU countries for business, cultural and tourism reasons. Similarly, more than half of the 32.8 million foreign nationals who entered Turkey in 2013 came from the United States and EU member countries.[6]

This economic picture has led the Turkish government and businesses to energetically advocate for Turkey's inclusion in TTIP. Turkish Prime Minister Recep Tayyip Erdogan wrote a personal letter on the subject to President Obama in April 2013 and Turkish Minister of Foreign Affairs Ahmet Davutoglu raised the issue with Secretary of State John Kerry during the latter's visit to Turkey in March 2013. Subsequently, Erdogan brought up the issue of TTIP and a possible bilateral free trade agreement with Obama during his visit to Washington in May. Similarly, Davutoglu raised the matter up once more with Kerry in Washington in November and also argued, in an article, that TTIP would help to anchor Turkey in the West.[7] In May 2014

---

[5]Data calculated from the Turkish Statistical Institute (TUIK) and the Turkish Central Bank.

[6]Data obtained from the General Directorate of Migration Management.

[7]Ahmet Davutoglu, "With the Middle East in Crisis, Turkey and the United States Must Deepen Alliance" *Foreign Policy*, November 15, 2014.

the new Turkish Minister of Economy Nihat Zeybekci met with his U.S. counterpart Michael Froman and then during his talk at Brookings Institution reiterated the importance that Turkey attributes to becoming part of TTIP.[8]

However, so far the question of Turkey's inclusion in TTIP remains unresolved. This chapter will argue that TTIP could indeed be a vehicle to revitalize and strengthen Turkey's ties with the transatlantic alliance. This is because beyond the economic advantages that Turkey can bring to the membership of TTIP,[9] the added value that Turkey can bring to the geopolitical objectives of TTIP must not be overlooked.

Just as Ukraine as well as Georgia and Moldova's future course has tremendous regional implications in terms of the strategic interests of the transatlantic community, so does that of Turkey. As a country sitting in the midst of a highly unstable and contested regions, the nature of Turkey's ties with the transatlantic community, including through TTIP, will impact significantly on Turkey's neighborhood. Turkey's exclusion from this new emerging international structure composed of TPP and TTIP risks pushing the country into the arms of those who challenge the Western economic and geopolitical order. It would also be damaging to Turkey's own economic development and democratization process. Instead, finding a way to include Turkey in TTIP, or alternatively signing a parallel free trade agreement between the United States and Turkey, would create a win-win situation for all involved—Turkey, the United States, the EU and Turkey's immediate neighborhood.

This chapter is divided into four sections. The first and second sections discuss the geopolitical dimension of TTIP and TTIP's potential impact on Turkey. The third section elaborates on the role that Turkey can play with respect to these objectives. The final section examines possible ways in which Turkey could be included or associated with TTIP.

---

[8]See: http://www.brookings.edu/events/2014/05/15-ttip-turkish-trade-economics-united-states.

[9]Discussed in some detail in my piece "Turkey and TTIP: Boosting the model partnership with the United States," *Turkey Project Policy Paper* (Washington DC: Center on the United States and Europe at Brookings Institution), No. 2, September 2013.

The Geopolitics of TTIP

At least three geopolitical and strategic objectives of TTIP can be cited. Beyond the immediate goal of taking economic relations to a new and higher level of interaction between the EU and the United States, both sides aspire to create the kind of political momentum needed to liberalize and reform the global economic system. EU and U.S. officials have not shied from openly expressing their hope and goal of using TTIP to unblock the WTO Doha negotiations and induce emerging countries in the longer run to adopt these WTO-plus standards, also sometimes referred to as the "new trade rulebook" for the 21st century.[10] They seek not only to dismantle remaining barriers to trade in goods and services, they want to standardize rules with respect to labor, environment, investment, competition policies and state-owned enterprises. These new standards would come to constitute a "state of the art" trade regime and set a precedent for future trade negotiations. These efforts could also encourage reluctant countries to come on board as the growing cost associated with being left out become apparent. This strategy, also sometimes characterized as the "tipping point strategy," aims to create a large integrated and liberalized market with high regulatory standards that would compel reluctant countries to adopt these standards to be able to enter and operate in the combined TPP and TTIP markets.[11]

Second, TTIP is also seen as a means to reinvigorating the transatlantic alliance at a time when traditional security and strategic issues have become less important to the relationship. The United States had played a critical role in the aftermath of World War II in reviving the European economy and assisting the initial steps of the European integration project. This was also accompanied by the establishment of NATO and the very close strategic cooperation achieved in countering the Soviet Union during the Cold War. The protection provided by NATO and the United States played a central role in the economic revival and growth of Western Europe. These developments

---

[10]Jeffrey J. Schott, Barbara Kotschwar, and Julia Muir, "Understanding the Trans-Pacific Partnership," *Policy Analyses in International Economics*, 99 (January 2013): pp. 11-12.

[11]Mireya Solis, "The Trans-Pacific Partnership: Can the United States Lead the Way in Asia-Pacific Integration?" *Pacific Focus: Inha Journal of International Studies*, 17, no. 3 (December 2012), p. 328.

were hailed as a sign of the emergence of a "security community" across the transatlantic.[12] After the end of the Cold War, the United States and EU member states continued to work very closely to ensure the enlargement of both the EU and NATO into central and Eastern Europe. After considerable tragedy, both sides were also able to cooperate very closely in stabilizing the Balkans and anchoring the region in the West.

However, U.S. involvement in the global war against terrorism, especially the intervention in Iraq and the infamous "pivot to Asia," complicated the relationship between the EU and the United States.[13] This was aggravated by the economic crisis and the enlargement fatigue that engulfed the EU. The EU became much more inward-looking and lost the ability to work together with the United States on geopolitical and strategic issues. The failure to respond decisively to the Color Revolutions in the post-Soviet republics and the failure to counter Russian intervention in Georgia in 2008 did result in geopolitical setbacks.

Beside the fact that TTIP is seen as a tool that can strengthen the economic performance of both parties it is increasingly also being seen as a project that would help to revive the geostrategic weight of the transatlantic alliance in world affairs. This may explain why some have spoken about TTIP as an "economic NATO."[14]

Third, TTIP is also considered to be a project that could reinforce "core values" of the Western liberal economic and political order such as the rule of law, human rights, and democratic governance. This ambitious objective indeed is somewhat reminiscent of the efforts after World War II and after the Cold War to restructure the interna-

---

[12]Karl W. Deutsch et al., *Political Community and the North Atlantic Area: International Organization in the Light of Historical Experience*, (Princeton: Princeton University Press, 1957).

[13]Nathalie Tocci and Riccardo Alcaro, "Three Scenarios for the Future of the Transatlantic Relationship," *Transworld Working Paper*, 04, September 2012.

[14]Numerous prominent personalities have employed this term. For instance, the Secretary General of NATO did so at an event at Brookings Institution in Washington DC, Transcripts of "The Future of the Alliance: Revitalizing NATO for a Changing World," featured speaker: Anders Fogh Rasmussen, March 19, 2014, http://www.brookings.edu/~/media/events/2014/3/19percent20rasmussenpercent20nato/20140319_nato_transcript.pdf, accessed May 15, 2014.

tional order. It comes also at a time when arguments about the "West" being in decline against the so-called "Rest" have been in vogue.[15] This is also accompanied by the more specific geopolitical struggles that are taking place in and over Ukraine, not to mention Georgia and Moldova. It is also possible to make similar remarks for Iraq and Syria, recognizing that the problems in both countries are much more serious and difficult. Hence, TTIP can also be seen as an effort to redress the balance in favor of a "weakened West" and the transatlantic community.[16] Clearly, such an achievement would considerably strengthen the geopolitical advantage that the "transatlantic form of governance" would enjoy in relations to the more authoritarian forms of governance represented by states such as China, Iran and Russia.

TTIP's Impact on Turkey

Existing impact studies evaluate only how trade will expand between the EU and the United States. The welfare gains for both sides are predicted to be very positive even if they vary depending on the nature of the agreement that might be reached. According to one such report prepared by the Centre for Economic Policy Research in London, the gains from a comprehensive liberalization of trade would be in the order of €119 billion for the United States and €95 billion for the EU per annum.[17] Another report prepared by the IFO Institute in Germany, in cooperation with the Bertelsmann Foundation, predicts substantive employment gains but notes that countries with preferential trade arrangements with the United States or the EU would be losers. Australia, Canada, Mexico and Turkey are highlighted as major losers resulting from trade diversion.[18]

---

[15]Charles A. Kupchan, *No One's World: The West, the Rising Rest, and the Coming Global Turn*, (Oxford: Oxford University Press, 2012).

[16]Daniel S. Hamilton, "America's Mega-Regional Trade Diplomacy: Comparing TPP and TTIP," *The International Spectator*, Vol. 49, No. 1, March 2014, p. 87.

[17]Joseph Francois, *Reducing Transatlantic Barriers to Trade and Investments: An Economic Assessment*, (London, UK: Center for Economic Policy Research, March 2013), p. 47.

[18]Gabriel Felbermayer et al., *Dimensions and Effects of a Transatlantic Free Trade Agreement Between the EU and the US*, German Federal Ministry of Economics and Technology (Munich, Germany: Ifo Institut, February 2013), p. 7. For an extended version of this study see Gabriel Felbermayer et al., *Transatlantic Trade and Partnership (TTIP): Who Benefits from a*

The fact that Turkey would experience a net loss of welfare is not surprising given the terms of its customs union with the EU. The customs union was negotiated with the expectation that it would be a transitional arrangement while Turkey moved towards eventual full membership in the EU, and that it would help to strengthen the Turkish economy in the meantime. Indeed, the customs union contributed greatly to Turkey's economic development and the competitiveness of its manufactured products. The adoption of EU regulatory standards and preferential access to the markets of EU members greatly benefitted Turkish economic development. The GDP of Turkey, according to IMF data, grew from $227.6 billion in 1995 to $ 827.2 billion in 2013. This is a 3.6-fold growth in nominal terms, and a significantly higher growth rate compared to that of the eurozone, which registered a 1.7-fold gain.[19]

However, this harmonization exercise also came with the requirement that Turkey adhere to the EU's common commercial policy. This has meant that each time the EU negotiates and signs a new free trade agreement with a third party, Turkey becomes bound by the terms of such an agreement. It then has to launch its own initiatives to conclude a similar agreement with that third party so as to acquire similar market access and eliminate the risk of a possible trade diversion. However, the absence of any provisions in the custom union that allows for Turkey to sit at the table during such negotiations or wield any tangible influence on the agreements themselves has created a very difficult situation in the long run. This difficulty has also been highlighted by the World Bank's report assessing the customs union between Turkey and the EU.[20]

In practice this has meant that Turkey has had to open up its market to export goods from these third parties without being granted reciprocal preferential access for Turkish goods. This puts Turkey at a

---

Free Trade Deal, GED Project Part 1: Macroeconomic Effects (Gutersloh, Germany: Bertelsmann Stiftung, June 2013). These studies should be considered as giving an approximate idea of the impact on Turkey and others.

[19]Calculated from data presented in *IMF World Economic Outlook*, April 2014, http://www.imf.org/external/pubs/ft/weo/2014/01/weodata/index.aspx, accessed in May 2014.

[20]*Evaluation of the EU TURKEY Customs Union*, (Washington DC: World Bank, March 28, 2014).

major disadvantage and results in possible trade diversion risks, especially when third parties refuse to negotiate and sign parallel free trade agreements with Turkey. This for example has long been the case with countries such Algeria, Mexico and South Africa after they signed their respective agreements with the EU in the early 2000s. Turkey has repeatedly approached these three countries to initiate negotiations to sign bilateral free trade agreements—to no avail. Similarly, Turkey is experiencing difficulties in engaging countries such as Canada, India, Japan and Vietnam that are in the process of negotiating their respective free trade agreements with the EU. This is leading to an increasing resentment against the customs union as well as questioning of relations with the EU by politicians and the public.

This problem is compounded by other Turkish grievances concerning the functioning of the customs union. One burning issue is the way in which Turkish business people have to be equipped with a visa to be able to travel in the EU.[21] This creates an extremely paradoxical situation where by the goods of Turkish companies circulate freely in the European internal market while producers face considerable hurdles when they wish to accompany those goods as part of regular business. This is in sharp contrast to European business people, who can travel to Turkey without visas and in the case of some nationalities even without passports. Similarly, there also complaints about limited transit quotas for trucks ferrying Turkish goods to EU member countries.[22] These two practices not only cause a lot of frustration among Turkish business people but also lead to allegations that both practices constitute a form of non-tariff barrier for Turkey's ability to export to the EU.

Hence, it is not surprising that some Turkish officials have been very critical of the customs union and the EU's reluctance to respond to their grievances. The former Minister of Economy, Zafer Çaglayan, as well as former Minister for EU Affairs, Egemen Bagis, expressed this frustration on a number of occasions when they publicly raised

---

[21]Kees Groenendijk and Elspeth Guild, *Visa Policy of Member States and the EU towards Turkish Nationals After Soysal,* (Istanbul: Economic Development Foundation, Publications No. 257, 2012).

[22]*An Analysis on the Impact of Road Transport Quotas: Submitted by the Government of the Republic of Turkey,* United Nations Economic and Social Council, ECE/TRANS/SC.1/2013/4, August 30, 2013.

the possibility of withdrawal from the customs union.[23] These declarations have come also against a background of growing disillusionment over Turkey's stalled EU accession process. Hence, it was not terribly surprising when Turkish Prime Minister Recep Tayyip Erdogan declared in January 2013 that he was ready to give up on EU membership and revealed that he had asked the Russian president, Vladimir Putin, if he could help with Turkey's admittance to the Shanghai Cooperation Organization (SCO).[24] In November 2013, during his visit to Russia, Erdogan renewed his call to join SCO and took it one step further by expressing interest to see Turkey become a member of the Eurasian customs union too:[25] the very union that a good part of the Ukrainian public loudly objects to joining. These feelings against the EU have also been shared by the wider public. In an opinion survey published in January 2013 by the Istanbul-based Center for Economic and Foreign Policy Studies (EDAM), only 33% of those surveyed thought Turkey should persist with membership in the next five years.[26] Their belief that EU membership being something good for the country was also down from 74% in 2004 to 44%, according to the Transatlantic Trends Survey of 2013.[27]

Would the Turkish Prime Minister realistically move Turkey away from the EU and out of the customs union, and redirect Turkey's eco-

---

[23]"Minister says Turkey to Reconsider EU Customs Union," *Today's Zaman*, March 25, 2013, accessed July 14, 2013, http://www.todayszaman.com/news-310708-minister-says-turkey-to-reconsider-eu-customs-union.html, "Revise Customs Union or Cancel it Totally," *Hurriyet Daily News*, March 28, 2013, http://www.hurriyetdailynews.com/revise-customs-union-or-cancel-it-totally—turkey-tells-eu.aspx?pageID=238&nid=43815 and "AB'ye Gumruk Birligi Uyarisi", *Sabah*, March 29, 2013, http://www.sabah.com.tr/Ekonomi/2013/03/29/abye-gumruk-birligi-uyarisi, accessed January, 2014

[24]Tayip Erdogan, *Sansürsüz Özel*, 24, (originally aired January 27, 2013), hosted by Yigit Bulut. Bulut has since been appointed as special advisor to the prime minister.

[25]*News conference following a meeting of the High-Level Russian-Turkish Cooperation Council*, November 22, 2013, http://eng.kremlin.ru/transcripts/6318 . For a commentary see "Erdogan's SCO, Eurasia Call May Represent No More Than Message to EU," *Today's Zaman*, December 1, 2013, http://www.todayszaman.com/newsDetail_openPrintPage.action?newsId=332721, accessed May, 2014.

[26]*Iliskilerin 50. Yilinda Avrupa Birligine Destek Azaliyor* [In the 50th year of relation support for the EU falling] January 2013, http://edam.org.tr/document/EDAMAnketOcak2013.pdf, accessed January 2014.

[27]*2013 Transatlantic Trends*, p. 46, http://trends.gmfus.org/files/2013/09/TTrends-2013-Key-Findings-Report.pdf, accessed January 2014.

nomic and political orientation away from the West and Western institutions? Probably not. Yet it goes without saying that the grievances held against the EU specifically and the West at large, including the United States, has been growing in recent times. Divergences between Turkey and its transatlantic allies on an ever-widening list of issues ranging from the crisis in Syria, the military coup in Egypt, relations with Israel and Hamas, and most recently the Turkish decision to purchase Chinese missiles, has become very conspicuous. However, the opening of a new chapter in EU-Turkish accession negotiations followed by Erdogan and Zeybekci's visits to Brussels in January and February 2014 together with the visit of Turkish Minister of Foreign Affairs, Ahmet Davutoglu to Washington DC in November as well as a series of ministers, are welcome developments and may well suggest a convergence in Western-Turkish positions actually driven at least partly by economic and trade considerations. Much more significant may well be that Zeybekci and his EU counterpart Karl de Gucht, the European Commissioner for Trade, started to explore the possibilities upgrading the customs union between the EU and Turkey.

However, the prospects of an exclusion from TTIP is highly likely to undermine this convergence process and aggravate Turkey's transatlantic relations because such an exclusion would mean that the United States would enjoy preferential access to the Turkish market without having to open up its market to Turkish exports.

Beyond unilateral U.S. access to Turkish markets, Turkish companies would become seriously disadvantaged by U.S. competitors who would benefit from more open access to the EU. These two developments would translate into loss of income as well as employment in Turkey, as predicted by the aforementioned impact studies, further aggravating the public's dissatisfaction with the EU, not to mention the United States. According to the Pew Global Attitudes Poll, in 2011 Turkish citizens gave the United States the lowest rating out of all the countries included in the survey at a staggeringly low 10% approval level, finishing behind a notoriously anti-American country as Pakistan. This trend pretty much continued in 2012 and 2013 with minor gains in favor of the United States. Given that such a level of public dissatisfaction is likely to be exploited by politicians in Turkey in a very populist manner, it would not be unrealistic to expect that

Turkey's commitment to the transatlantic alliance would suffer adversely.

Yet, this does not necessarily need to be the case. Large business interest groups, such as the Independent Industrialists and Businessmen's Association (MUSIAD), the Turkish Union of Chambers and Commodity Exchanges (TOBB), the Turkish Industrialists' and Businessmen's Association (TUSIAD) and the Turkish Confederation of Businessmen and Industrialists (TUSKON) have repeatedly underlined the importance of Turkey's Western orientation and its relations with the EU as critical to its economic growth and performance. The survey by EDAM mentioned earlier on also revealed that when a panel of 202 experts was questioned about EU-Turkish relations almost 87% supported the view that Turkey should persist with pursuing EU membership. Clearly better informed opinion much better appreciates the importance of the EU for Turkey.

Often these are also the very circles that are keen to get Turkey involved in TTIP. They are aware that if Turkey were to become part of TTIP there would be upfront technical costs associated with implementing new regulatory standards, and political costs resulting from populist criticism directed at the requirement of adopting rules without having had a chance to shape them. At the same time, they also recognize that the cost of being left outside TTIP, accompanied with a weakening of relations with the EU, would be even higher, both economically and politically. This is clearly noted by a 2013 report prepared by the Economic Policy Research Foundation of Turkey (TEPAV) a think-tank closely associated with TOBB.[28]

Turkey's Potential Contribution to TTIP's Economic and Geopolitical Objectives

Inclusion of Turkey in TTIP or some accompanying arrangement would visibly contribute to TTIP's economic as well as geopolitical and strategic goals. The Turkish economy has dramatically transformed in the course of the last two to three decades. Once dominated

---

[28]Bozkurt Aran, "Global Partnership Quests: New Contentious Dynamics in Trade and Prospects for Turkey in an Age of TPP and TTIP," *Turkish Policy Brief Series*, Eleventh Edition, 2013.

by agriculture and an import substitution industry, the economy is now driven by services and an export-oriented manufacturing sector. One important aspect of this transformation is that foreign trade has acquired a much greater place in Turkey's GDP compared to the past. In 1975, foreign trade accounted for only 9% of Turkey's GDP. In 2012 this figure had increased to 50%. Turkish foreign trade increased from around $6.1 billion in 1975 to about $403 billion in 2013.[29] Turkey has become deeply integrated with the global economy, particularly with the EU and its immediate neighborhood. In 2013, Turkey was the 6th largest trading partner of the EU, just ahead of Japan and Brazil, but behind Norway and Switzerland.[30] These developments suggest that, even if at a modest level, Turkey as a trading and investment partner to the EU and the United States can contribute to economic growth and employment in the transatlantic community.

The demographic advantages that Turkey enjoys when compared to the aging and declining population in the EU point to a likely growth in such a contribution. In turn, inclusion in TTIP would surely give an additional push to the Turkish economy's growth and further strengthen the Turkish economy's potential contribution as a source of growth and employment. This would not be limited to the EU and the United States but also benefit countries in its immediate neighborhood. A Turkey in TTIP would be a Turkey with a greater economy. This would translate into Turkey becoming a greater importer of the goods and services of neighboring countries and hence a source of economic growth and employment from them too. Actually, during the last two decades the biggest gains in foreign trade were achieved with Turkey's immediate neighborhood: trade expanded from about $4 billion in 1992 to $92.8 billion in 2012, a 23-fold increase compared to a 9-fold and 6-fold increase, respectively, for trade with the EU and the United States during the same period.[31]

---

[29]Data calculated from TUIK.

[30]"Client and Supplier Countries of the EU28 in Merchandise Trade (value percent)," http://trade.ec.europa.eu/doclib/docs/2006/september/tradoc_122530.pdf, accessed May 2014.

[31]For a discussion of Turkey's trade with its neighborhood see Kemal Kirişci, "Turkey and Its Post-Soviet Neighborhood", *Current History*, Vol. 112, No. 756, October 2013 and Kemal Kirişci, "Arab Uprisings and Completing Turkey's Regional Economic Integration: Challenges and Opportunities for US-Turkish Relations" *Journal of Balkan and Near East Studies*, Vol. 15, No. 2, 2013.

Turkish business presence and investments in these neighboring countries, such as Bulgaria, Romania, Russia, Georgia and Iraq, also greatly expanded in the course of the last two decades. These investments include bakeries and restaurants set up by individuals, as well as manufacturing plants by major Turkish companies. Turkish Central Bank figures suggest that Turkish FDI stock in neighboring countries increased from just about $900 million in 2001 to $6.5 billion in 2012. It is widely acknowledged that the real figure is much larger than the one quoted by the Central Bank. This suggests that Turkey is already directly contributing to the economic growth of neighboring countries through investment too. Inclusion in TTIP would expand this impact. Furthermore, although there are no known studies it should also be possible to argue that Turkey's economic engagement in its neighborhood in turn also indirectly contributes to demand for both EU and U.S. goods, services and investments in this region. An already existing manifestation of this development is that a growing number of American and European companies are basing their regional operations in Turkey. Turkey's inclusion in TTIP is likely to strengthen this direct and indirect effect resulting from Turkey's economic engagement of its neighborhood to the benefits of all parties involved. Turkey's engagement with its neighborhood can also contribute to TTIP's strategic objectives in two distinctive ways. Turkish trade and investment can help to ease at least parts of the neighborhood into a Western liberal economic order. Actually, Davutoglu actively sought to develop such an order through encouraging greater regional economic integration through the signing of free trade agreements and liberalization of visas.[32] Second, as mentioned earlier, Turkey straddles a region where Eizenstat's two forms of governance meet and compete with each other. This competition is most conspicuous over Ukraine, but it also involves Armenia, Georgia and Moldova. Turkey economic relations with Ukraine had been expanding until recently, and Turkey is Georgia's leading economic partner. There is also a modest amount of trade and business relations occurring between Armenia and Turkey in spite of the border between the countries being closed.[33]

---

[32]Ibid.

[33]Kemal Kirişci and Andrea Moffatt, "A Turkish-Armenian Rapprochement?" *National Interest*, May 2, 2014, http://nationalinterest.org/commentary/turkish-armenian-rapprochement-10373?page=show.

Turkey's engagement with this neighborhood serves at least three important functions. First, the Turkish economy is a liberal market economy and inevitably Turkish commercial actors become vehicles in disseminating rules and values associated with a liberal market economy.[34] These actors have a stake in operating in an environment of rule of law and as they seek such an environment they socialize their counterparts into such values. It should also be remembered that many of these Turkish commercial actors interact with especially the EU and operate with the rules and standards that govern the customs union between Turkey and the EU.

Second, Turkey, even if modestly, helps to diminish the dependence of these economies on Russia and becomes a kind of a conveyor belt connecting them into global markets. In contrast to any other major economy in this neighborhood—such as Russia and Iran—Turkey is the only one that is most closely and deeply integrated with the Western liberal economic order. Inclusion of Turkey in TTIP would not only deepen Turkey's involvement in this liberal order but also increase its role in helping to ease its neighborhood into this order.

Third, Turkey could help reduce the EU's energy dependency on Russia. The crisis in Ukraine and the annexation of Crimea has suddenly brought back the geopolitical reality of the EU's energy dependency on Russia. There is now even talk of including an energy chapter in TTIP negotiation as part of a transatlantic effort to reduce some of its dependency. Turkey itself is heavily dependent especially on Russian gas and is trying to diversify its energy sources. It has reached an agreement to construct Trans-Anatolian Gas Pipeline (TANAP) and obtain Azeri gas. Turkey also signed deals with the Kurdistan Regional Government (KRG) to import energy even if for the time being the implementation of this deal is being held up by the central government in Iraq. The discovery of natural gas deposits in Eastern Mediterranean has raised the prospects of some of this gas being sent to Turkey and on to Europe. These developments if successfully managed could clearly help diversify EU energy supplies and improve the EU's dependency on Russia. Actually, Turkey aspires to

---

[34]Kemal Kirişci, "Democracy Diffusion: the Turkish Experience" in Linden, Ronald (et al.) *Turkey and Its Neighbors: Foreign Relations in Transition*, (Boulder, Colorado: Lyne Rienner, 2011).

become both a transit and hub for energy reliable flows between alternative suppliers to Russia and Europe.[35]Following the Russian military intervention in Georgia in 2008 and Russian unilateral sanctions against Georgia, it is difficult to see how Georgia could have maintained its links with the West and sustained its aspirations to become part of the transatlantic community if it did not have Turkey next door. The impact of the crisis on Turkey's role with respect to Ukraine is still not very clear. Turkey like a number of EU member countries has been somewhat subdued in its response to Russia in an effort to protect its commercial and economic interests there. At the same time there is also deep seated concern about Ukraine's territorial integrity and the geopolitical consequences of its violation. Ukraine and Turkey were negotiating a free trade agreement to deepen economic integration between the two countries and visa requirements had been lifted reciprocally. However, when and if a pro-Western Ukrainian government does consolidate power in Kyiv, its economic relations with Turkey is likely to carry geopolitical significance in terms of alleviating some of its dependence on Russia. It is also possible that if Turkey had closer and more normal relations with Armenia, the Armenian government might have not felt that dependent on Russia and not been compelled to suspend its negotiations with the EU and accept to join the Eurasian customs union.

The place where Turkey's role as a conveyer belt for bringing a country into the global economy and attach it to Western liberal economic order is most visible is the Kurdistan region of Iraq. After long years of difficult relations with Kurds both inside the country and in northern Iraq the current Turkish government has not only adopted policies to try to improve the situation of Kurds in Turkey but also dramatically ameliorated and expanded relations with the Kurdistan Regional Government (KRG).[36] Turkey's economic engagement of this region of Iraq and close relations with KRG have not only brought the region much closer to the West, but also spared the region from the instability and violence that persists in the rest of Iraq.

---

[35]Gareth Winrow, "Realization of Turkey's Energy Aspirations: Pipe Dreams or Real Projects?" *Turkey Project Policy Paper*, (Center on the United States and Europe at Brookings Institution), No. 4, April 2014.

[36]Henry Barkey, "Turkey's New Engagement in Iraq: Embracing Iraqi Kurdistan," *United States Institute of Peace: Special Report*, No. 237, May 2010.

A similar argument could also be made with respect to TTIP's "tipping point strategy" of encouraging challengers among emerging markets to adopt the new WTO-plus standards to be embodied in TTIP and TPP to enjoy market access. TTIP would institute an integrated market covering a geographic area stretching from the Pacific coast of the United States to the western shores of the Black Sea, with TPP expanding this zone to a good part of the Pacific basin. Turkey would be one of the few major liberal market economies standing between the two ends of this integrated region yet not included in the agreements. While its exclusion risks pushing Turkey closer to emerging markets resisting WTO-plus standards, the exact opposite would be the case in the event of Turkey's inclusion. Additionally, Turkey would be able to bring the weight of those parts of its neighborhood that would have already adopted some rules and the frame of mind associated with WTO-plus standards. Surely, the "tipping point strategy" would enjoy a greater likelihood of working if a long-standing member of the Western liberal economic order was on board.

Finally, the inclusion of Turkey would also help to consolidate and strengthen democratic governance in Turkey. The EU played a critical role in the democratization of Turkey. However, in the course of the last year Turkey's democracy has been facing growing challenges. There are many who believe that there is a relationship between the deterioration of EU-Turkish relations together with the weakening of Turkey's prospects of membership being at least one important factor contributing to the recent democratic setbacks in the country. Even if at times the thesis is contested that economic growth and liberal market policies help to expand middle classes and democracy, it would be difficult to dismiss this thesis completely in the case of Turkey. The growth of a liberal market and accompanying middle class continues to be seen as a factor that helped democratization in Turkey. In the absence of an EU perspective, Turkey's inclusion in TTIP would give a boost to economic growth and to the process of strengthening the middle class. In turn this would contribute to the additional objective of promoting and strengthening the "core values" of the Western liberal economic and political order in Turkey as well as in Turkey's neighborhood. It is not surprising that during the initial stages of the Arab Spring Turkey's economic success received considerable attention and the link between this performance and Turkey's democracy was widely recognized. This would also be in line with the long standing strategic goals of the United States and the EU of supporting a democratic and liberal Turkey as a pole of attraction and stability in its neighborhood.

How to Engage Turkey in TTIP

Now that TTIP negotiations have formally started, including Turkey at the table does not seem like an option. Initially, this course of action was suggested by Turkish officials and business people and they actively lobbied various EU governments as well as the European Commission in this vein. The Turkish side even tried to mobilize U.S. government support to get Turkey involved in TTIP, but to no avail. These lobbying efforts were ultimately rejected on the grounds that Turkey is not a member of the EU. The most that the Turkish side could receive were assurances that they would be informed regularly about relevant developments in TTIP negotiations.

There are also those in Turkey who have advocated that Turkey could be included in the final agreement on TTIP on the grounds of the customs union and the EU membership process. This is a method that is preferred especially by those in Turkey who fear that Congressional politics would not allow the ratification process of a separate trade agreement with the United States to go through. However, this too is highly unlikely to take place, and even if it did it would mean Turkey having to accept all the terms of the agreement without being party to the negotiations. Another alternative is to write into TTIP the possibility for third countries to accede to the agreement after the fact. TTIP could be left open to countries that have long standing trade agreements with the United States or the EU. Countries such as Canada, Mexico, Norway and Switzerland together with Turkey have been mentioned.

Known also as "docking," this is a provision that the United States has advocated for in the context of TPP negotiations. For this to be an option, TTIP would need to have the required clauses within the agreement, and Turkey's application would need to be accepted. The downside for such an arrangement for Turkey is that accession would most likely require Congressional as well as EU approval and this may well complicate the process. Similar to the previous option here to there would be complications especially with respect to domestic politics resulting from having to adopt all the obligations of the treaty without the possibility of negotiating any of the terms. Nevertheless, by introducing transition periods for the implementation of some of the more demanding terms, this could prove to be a manageable exercise. However, it would be very important that this process not turn into an experience similar to the one with the EU. A long and drawn-out accession process would be a recipe for disaster in Turkey's relations with its transatlantic allies. In the meantime there are no immediate signs of an effort on the part of the aforementioned countries to pool their resources to develop a common position with respect to TTIP or for that matter "docking." Furthermore, for the time being the Turkish side considers its position to be considerably different than the others because of the customs union, and hence has not engaged those countries that have free trade arrangements with the EU or the United States.

Another approach would be to revisit the possibility of negotiating and signing an independent free trade agreement between Turkey and the United States. Expanding economic relations between the two countries have been advocated for some time. Madeleine Albright and Steven Hadley proposed an ambitious plan in 2011 in the form of a "Turkish-American Partnership" that would incorporate "the TPP's emphasis on market access, regulatory compatibility, business facilitation, assistance for small and medium-sized enterprises, and promotion of trade in cutting-edge technologies."[37] The idea appears to have never been seriously pursued because of the restrictions placed on Turkey's ability to negotiate and conclude free trade agreements independently of its customs union with the EU. Now that TTIP is being negotiated, such a restriction would no longer be applicable. However, one challenge here, if such an agreement were to mirror TTIP, is that this agreement would inevitably cover sectors not included in the customs union, such as agriculture, services, or government procurement. This would create a curious situation in which the agreement with the United States would go beyond the terms of the customs union with

---

[37]Madeleine K. Albright and Stephen Hadley, *US-Turkey Relations: A New Partnership*, Independent Task Force Report no. 69 (New York, NY: Council on Foreign Relations, 2012), p. 13.

the EU, possibly creating complications to EU-Turkish relations and also raising possible legal challenges to whether the customs union agreement would allow for such an FTA between Turkey and the United States. However, this could also be an opportunity for strengthening EU-Turkish relations. Most of the areas that would be covered by TTIP beyond the customs union are actually areas that are part of the stalled EU-Turkish accession process. In other words, these are the very regulatory areas that Turkey needs to address to align more closely with the EU. Furthermore, the World Bank report mentioned earlier actually recommends that both the EU and Turkey revisit the customs union and look into ways of enhancing this relationship by addressing, *inter alia*, the above issues areas.

The Turkish side has been pushing energetically the idea of a free trade agreement with the U.S. side especially during Prime Minister Erdogan's visit to Washington DC. However, the idea did not gain enough traction with the U.S. administration and the Turkish side had to settle for what a disappointed Turkish diplomat called "yet another committee." Concerns ranging from an already loaded trade agenda, congressional politics and democratic setbacks in Turkey appear to have played a role in this decision. Instead, the Turkish side accepted the establishment of a High Level Committee, to be led by the Ministry of Economy of Turkey and the Office of the U.S. Trade Representative, with the ultimate objective of continuing to deepen the economic relations and liberalize trade as well as examine the impact that TTIP could have on Turkey.[38] Nevertheless, on the Turkish side there is some hope that this committee might evolve to something like the High Level Working Group between the EU and the United States, which eventually recommended the negotiation of TTIP. In this way the Committee would constitute a governmental forum where both sides could discuss and ripen the idea of a free trade agreement. This of course would need to be accompanied by a bottom-up process of mobilization coming from the business world. Clearly, the broader the basis of demand for deeper economic relations with Turkey, the greater would be the likelihood of achieving the public support needed to negotiate a free trade agreement. But the enthusiasm of

---

[38]Fact Sheet: U.S.-Turkey Economic Partnership", The White House Office of the Press Secretary, May 16, 2013, accessed July 12, http://www.whitehouse.gov/the-press-office/2013/05/16/fact-sheet-us-turkey-economic-partnership.

Turkish and American businesses must be matched by a genuine will in government and congressional circles.

Against this limited list of options, the least that could be encouraged is greater trilateral consultations at two levels. The first level would be inter-governmental. Officials from the European Commission and possibly also interested member countries, the United States and Turkey would meet regularly to discuss the developments with respect to TTIP negotiations. This would give a chance to the Turkish side to follow developments especially with respect to regulatory issues and be able to do their homework. Additionally such a consultation mechanism would in itself become a major confidence-building exercise—an exercise direly needed in this triangular relationship. An immediate issue that could also be addressed is the inclusion of Turkey in impact studies commissioned by the EU and the United States. The initial study commissioned by the EU did not include Turkey. Since then the Commission has responded favorably to calls to have Turkey included in the overall study of TTIP's impact scheduled to be completed by the end of 2014.[39]

A second trilateral consultation mechanism could operate in the form of second track diplomacy involving academics, former officials and business people. The purpose of this level of consultation would be to explore ideas and ways to involve Turkey in TTIP and prepare briefings and reports for the first level inter-governmental consultations. A more ambitious version of these consultations could include participation from other major members of the Western liberal economic order such as Canada, Mexico, Norway and Switzerland.

Conclusion

TTIP and TPP will profoundly impact the international economic order. The Western liberal order that was put into place at the end of World War II has faced growing challenges from emerging countries.

---

[39] *Trade Sustainability Impact Assessment on TTIP between the EU and the USA* commissioned by the European Commission. The final version of the report is to be published by the end of 2014 and promises to report in detail the effects of TTIP on Turkey too, *Final Inception Report*, April 28, 2014, p. 23, http://www.trade-sia.com/ttip/wp-content/uploads/sites/6/2014/02/TSIA-TTIP-Final-Inception-Report-.pdf, accessed May 2014.

Beyond immediate economic growth and employment-related objectives, TPP and TTIP also aim to reinvigorate the Western liberal order by creating a new generation of regulatory standards to govern trade and investments. This is accompanied by an understanding that third countries interested in accessing these two markets will need to adopt these standards. TPP and especially TTIP is also about reinforcing "core values" of the transatlantic governance model, with its emphasis on the rule of law, human rights and democracy. Interestingly this is occurring at a time when emerging economies appear to be losing their edge and dynamism over the established economies and democracies. Hence, TTIP and TPP together may indeed succeed both economically as well as strategically in reinforcing the Western liberal economic as well as political order.

In the course of the last two to three decades, Turkey has been deeply transformed both economically and politically. Turkey's close relations with the EU and the United States have made an important contribution to this process. In turn Turkey has continued to be an important ally of the United States in an increasingly volatile region. Turkey came to be praised for its soft power and has also been presented as a model for the transformation of the Middle East. However, in recent years Turkey has entered a period where its commitment and ties to this transatlantic community is being questioned and its economy is showing signs of strains. This is occurring at a time when the United States is negotiating TTIP and TPP, two agreements that promise to achieve greater economic integration among countries who produce almost two thirds of the world's GDP and half its trade. It also coincides with a period when Turkey's neighborhood is in a state of turmoil and the influence of the transatlantic community is being energetically contested. This can be seen not just in Syria and Iraq but also in the post-Soviet world and most obviously in Ukraine.

Where should Turkey be? In the course of the last couple of years its relations with the EU and the United States have not been the best. A long list of grievances has piled up, especially with respect to the operation of the customs union and the EU membership process. More recently, Turkey had tended to see developments in the Middle East from an increasingly different perspective than the United States. At times these differences have turned out to be very bitter. However, Turkey may well be at a crossroads. The Middle East has not turned into the economically promising and political stable reform-oriented geography that many had hoped when the Arab Spring first broke out. Instead the region is in a deep state of turmoil, and the worst chaos is on Turkey's doorstep. Recent developments have also shown that Turkey is unable to shape these events the way it prefers on its own. Much worse is that the instability next door is at the brink of spilling over into Turkey. This may well be a critical moment when Turkey has to make a choice somewhat similar to the one it made at the end of World War II and the beginning of the Cold War when it made the strategic decision to reinforce its ties with the West. These two decisions served Turkey well, how could one otherwise explain that Turkey is doing so much better than those countries that chose differently. Furthermore, reinvigorating ties with the West does not mean abandoning the Middle East or its immediate neighborhood. On the contrary, all the evidence from the last decade or so is that the neighborhood prefers to see a Turkey with strong ties to the West and especially to the EU. A strong signal and commitment on the part of Turkey in support of its ties with the West surely would contribute positively to the efforts of those who would want to see Turkey in TTIP.

The EU and the United States will need to do their share too. There is growing recognition that Turkish economic development has reached the point where Turkey can make a difference to the economic growth and employment levels in the United States and the EU, not to mention its neighborhood. This is accompanied also by a recognition that strategically keeping Turkey in the West and as a member of the transatlantic alliance is in the interest of both the EU and the United States. However, what is needed is a corresponding will and policy determination to engage Turkey accordingly and not take Turkey for granted. This would require a vision somewhat similar to the one that existed in the United States in the latter parts of the 1940s and in the then European Economic Community exactly half a century ago, when an association agreement was signed with Turkey with the clear understanding that Turkey would become a member of what subsequently became the EU. Such a vision would help to open up new horizons with respect to TTIP and TTIP could become the project for the 21st century for re-anchoring Turkey in the transatlantic community.

How would have the history of the Cold War unfolded had U.S. decision-makers in the late 1940s not launched the Truman Doctrine, supported the inclusion of Turkey in NATO and left Turkey outside the transatlantic alliance? This is the kind of question to which one would not be able to provide a convincing answer. Yet, the least that can be said is that the geopolitics of Turkey's neighborhood would probably have evolved along very different lines. The issue of whether Turkey should or should not be part of TTIP is a question of a similar caliber. This is not very different from asking oneself how the crisis in Syria would have looked like had EU-Turkish relations remained on course and Turkey had joined the EU together with Croatia. This clearly is a speculative issue, but it is the opinion of this author that the situation in Syria would at least not be worse than it is today.

A similar question could also be asked about Armenia. Would Armenia have been compelled to join the Russian-led Eurasian customs union and lend its support to the results of the referendum in Crimea? Again it is the opinion of this author that most probably Armenia would be on track with its association process with the EU easing itself out of the grip of Russia. Such a question can be raised for Ukraine too. In other words, whether Turkey remains tightly anchored in the West or not has regional geopolitical and strategic consequences. The issue of Turkey's inclusion into TTIP is of similar significance. Turkey can hugely benefit from membership to TTIP, as it did from the customs union, but much more importantly the dynamics of the Turkish economy, the geographical location of Turkey, the demography of Turkey, the political system of Turkey, Turkey's continuing, against all odds, close and intense connection to the transatlantic community can benefit TTIP economically, geopolitically and strategically.

The key is to mobilize the will to find a way to include or associate Turkey with TTIP. The winners would be the EU, the United States, Turkey's neighborhood, and clearly Turkey itself, but also Eizenstat's "transatlantic model" of governance. This is when TTIP's geopolitical and strategic objectives would fully be served.

The Transatlantic Trade and Investment Partnership in the Global Context

Michael G. Plummer

The EU and the U.S. economies are the largest in the world and their bilateral ties constitute the most important bilateral economic relationship. Moreover, the United States and European countries have been key leaders in post-World War II economic governance and in promoting liberalization of global trade and investment. They have among the lowest tariffs and non-tariff barriers (NTBs) in the world; they have low barriers to inward and outward foreign direct investment (FDI); and their respective competition policies, intellectual property protection, and political and economic institutions are among the most advanced. By almost every measure, they would be considered "like-minded," as demonstrated by the membership of the United States and many European nations in the OECD and their leadership in the World Trade Organization (WTO) and other fora.

Yet, despite this extensive integration and generally a common policy stance, the United States and the EU do not have a formal free trade area (FTA) in place. Twenty years ago, this was very understandable; the Uruguay Round, which created the WTO, was finalized in 1994 and was a major priority for both; the United States (and the world) had not yet embraced regionalism as an important part of its commercial policy strategy and had actually been a multilateral "purist" (more or less) until the mid-1980s, after which it only put in place a few minor FTAs and eventually NAFTA in 1993; the EU was busy implementing its Single Market Programme and its attention was captured by monetary union and enlargement toward the East after the 1989 revolutions; new excitement was created by emerging markets especially in Asia; and growth in the OECD economies in the 1990s was strong. And these are just economic reasons.

Nevertheless, the changes in the global economy that began in the 1980s in favor of greater globalization intensified over the next two decades, and with the advent of the 21st century, the world transformed significantly. The gravity of the global economy began to shift away from the OECD countries in favor of emerging markets in Asia and elsewhere; the sleeping "Asian Giants" of China and India awoke during this period, and China in particular took off in a spectacular fashion, rising to be the second largest (single) economy in the world and eventually its biggest exporter. Although the Doha Development Agenda (DDA) was launched in November 2001, FTAs became the driving force in international commercial policy. As of January 31, 2014 the WTO reported that, counting goods and services separately, it had received 583 notifications of regional trading arrangements (RTAs, defined by the WTO to be a reciprocal trading agreement between two or more countries), with 377 in force.[1] This number is up from 300 at the end of 2005 and 130 at the beginning of 1995.[2] At the same time, the DDA has generally reached an impasse. Although at the WTO's Ninth Ministerial Meeting in Bali in December 2013 members succeeded in delivering the first liberalization package since the launch of the Doha Development Agenda in 2001, including agreements pertinent to trade facilitation, agriculture, and development-related issues, the results are modest for 12 years of negotiations and the "single undertaking" is still on hold.

The United States and the EU have now both become active in the regionalism movement, but did not start bilateral negotiations in favor of a formal FTA until the launch of the Transatlantic Trade and Investment Partnership (TTIP) talks in July 2013. The timing is not coincidental. The United States has been active in cementing closer relations with its partners particularly in the Asia-Pacific region, beginning with the Bush Administration and then folded into the "Asian pivot" of the Obama Administration. The greatest manifestation of this has been the push toward the creation of a "Trans-Pacific Partnership" (TPP). The TPP agreement negotiations were launched

---

[1]WTO website, www.wto.org, accessed June 14, 2014.

[2]Michael G. Plummer, "Toward Win-Win Regionalism in Asia: Issues and Challenges in Forming Efficient Trade Agreements, Asian Development Bank, Office of Regional Economic Integration, *Working Paper Series on Regional Economic Integration No. 5*, pp. 1-57, October 2006.

in 2008 and the 20th round of negotiations took place in February 2014. The TPP builds on a high-quality FTA between four small, open economies (Brunei Darussalam, Singapore, New Zealand and Chile), known as the "P4," and in addition to these negotiating parties the TPP includes the United States, Australia, Malaysia, Vietnam, Peru, Canada, Mexico, and, as of July 2013, Japan, i.e., the same month when TTIP was launched. South Korea, which already has an FTA in place with both the EU and the United States, is currently undertaking preliminary talks with TPP countries with a view possibly to join. The Philippines, Thailand, and Indonesia have all expressed interest in possibly joining; China is also considering the possibility at a future date.[3]

The TPP is distinct in terms of not only large differences in levels of development but also its ambitions to become a modern, "21st century" agreement that would embrace a wide variety of areas, including border and non-border barriers to trade in goods and services, FDI, intellectual property protection, trade facilitation, competition policy, and even sections on science and technology and small- and medium-sized enterprises. As such, it aims to create a system of global rules that would be applicable beyond the Asia-Pacific region.

This last point is particularly important. The TPP and "mega-regionalism" in the Asia-Pacific is not a big threat to the EU in the traditional sense of trade and investment diversion; one study[4] estimates that a successful TPP would lead to trade diversion of $3.4 billion by 2025, just a blip in a projected EU economy of $22.7 trillion. Adding prospective Asian economies like China to the group actually would lead to a slight increase in EU income ($900 million), due to associated open reforms and greater growth in the region.[5] Rather, the risk is that the EU will be isolated from rule-making, and centrifugal forces of regionalism could work to the disadvantage of EU produc-

---

[3]Peter A. Petri, Michael G. Plummer, and Fan Zhai, "The TPP, China, and FTAAP: The Case for Convergence," forthcoming publication of the China Pacific Economic Cooperation Council (China PECC), 2014. Available at: http://papers.ssrn.com/sol3/papers.cfm?abstract_id=2438725 .

[4]Peter A. Petri, Michael G. Plummer, and Fan Zhai, *The Trans Pacific Partnership and Asia-Pacific Integration: A Quantitative Assessment.* Washington, DC: Peterson Institute for International Economics, November 2012.

[5]Petri, et. al. 2014, *op. cit.*

tion networks in the region. In terms of the former risk, the downfall of the "Anti-Counterfeiting Trade Agreement" (ACTA) is a case in point. Together with the United States and other economies, the European Commission (EC) had a hand in crafting ACTA and it was signed by the EC in July 2012. However, it was subsequently rejected by the European Parliament. The industry, therefore, has now been looking to the intellectual property protection chapter in the TPP, in which the EC has no direct influence. If new global rules are created by this mega-regionalism movement, it would make sense from a European perspective to be part of it.

The same might be said of the Regional Comprehensive Economic Partnership (RCEP) agreement, launched in November 2012. It is the first major initiative that has been spearheaded by ASEAN as part of its strategy of "ASEAN Centrality"; indeed, membership in RCEP is open only to economies that have an existing FTA with ASEAN, that is, China, Japan, South Korea, Australia, New Zealand, and India. It, too, is intended to be a "high quality" agreement, though its focus on being more "flexible" than the TPP—as well as its membership— suggests that it will be less comprehensive. The leaders of RCEP have given themselves until 2015 to complete an agreement. Like TTIP, there is no doubt that the creation of RCEP is being pushed by the TPP, with China being an important actor in that agreement whereas it is not (at least as yet) been in the TPP. While RCEP has a long way to go, it also still has the potential to be influential, particularly since it would envision free trade in Northeast Asia (the key economic space in Asia but where economic relations are hampered by bad history and politics) and India, by far the largest country in South Asia.

The goal of this chapter is to consider the economic and policy implications of the TTIP in the context of this rapidly-changing global environment. The rest of the chapter is organized as follows. Section II gives a brief review of the transatlantic trade and invest-ment relationship, followed in Section III by analysis of the economics of TTIP. Finally, Section IV considers TTIP in view of the changing global policy landscape, particularly in view of the "mega-regionalism" trend in the Asia-Pacific region.

Brief Review of the EU-U.S. Economic Relationship

While the EU-U.S. economic relationship is in many ways the most important in the world, regional economic cooperation initiatives, the rise of Asia and emerging markets as major players in the international marketplace, and relatively low growth rates have combined to reduce the importance of the bilateral relationship, at least at the margin. According to OECD data, the United States accounts for 23% of total EU exports and 21% of total imports on a value added basis, whereas the EU receives 29% of U.S. exports and accounts for 27% of U.S. imports on a value-added basis.[6] Hence, each party is the other's most important trading partner. The share of value-added in services between the partners is significantly higher, and is also higher than in each partner's trade with the rest of the world.[7] However, the share is falling somewhat: much earlier data are not available in value added terms but in nominal terms over the 2000–2012 period, the share of the EU (U.S.) in U.S. (EU) exports has fallen from 22% (28%) to 17% (17%) (Figures 1 and 2). To a large degree the drop in transatlantic shares has reflected an increase in the importance of the Chinese markets, whose share has increased four-fold in the case of EU exports (2% to 8% percent) and three-fold in the case of U.S. exports (3% to 9%).[8]

In terms of FDI, the United States and the EU are far and away each the other's most important external investment partner. In 2012, almost two-thirds (65%) of the inward FDI flows in the United States was of EU origin, while 45% of the U.S. outward flows went to the EU (Figure 3). These shares continue to be dominant but have been falling somewhat over time; in 2000, FDI flows to the EU constituted a slightly higher share of total U.S. outward FDI (50%) and inward

---

[6]These data are reported in the OECD/WTO "trade in value added" database (http://stats.oecd.org/Index.aspx?DataSetCode=TIVA_OECD_WTO). Using value added gives a much better indication of actual economic integration relative to nominal flows, which are subject to "double counting" and other biases.

[7]OECD, "The Transatlantic Trade and Investment Partnership: Why Does it Matter?" June, 2013.

[8]While China's share of U.S. and EU imports has not grown as impressively as that of exports, it is still larger for both countries, i.e., China accounted for 16% of EU imports and 19% of U.S. imports, i.e., a larger share in the latter case than the EU (*IMF Direction of Trade Statistics*).

Figure 1. Direction of U.S. Exports, 2012 and 2000, Selected Countries

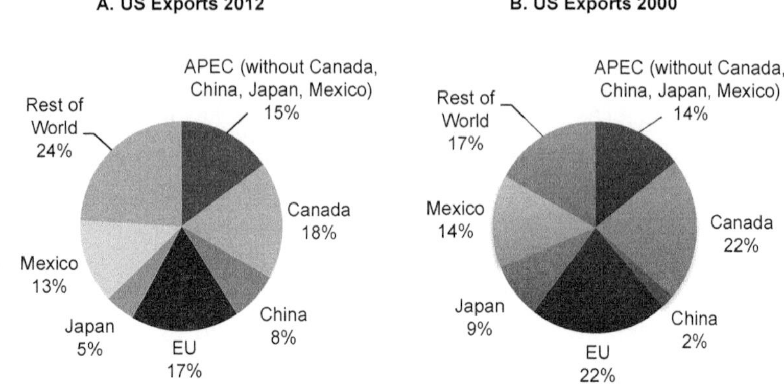

Source: IMF Direction of Trade Statistics.

Figure 2. Direction of EU Exports, 2012 and 2000, Selected Countries

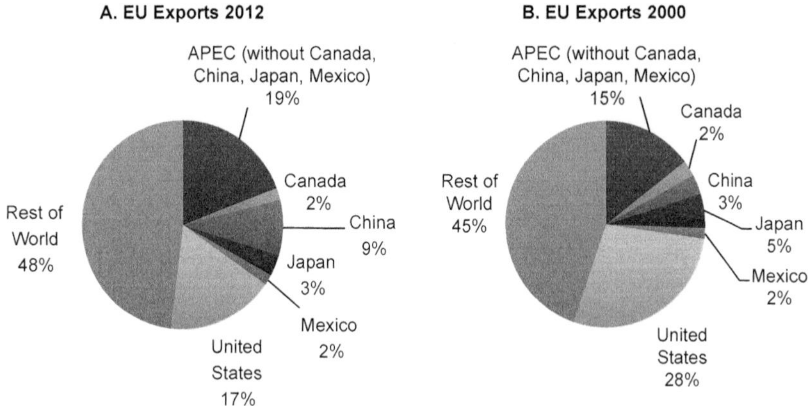

Source: IMF Direction of Trade Statistics.

flows from the EU represented 75% of the total (Figure 3). In terms of shares of EU FDI flows (Figure 4), intra-EU FDI obviously dominates, but otherwise the United States is the single most destination/source of FDI flows; over the period 2000–2012, the share of the United States in EU inward flows has been rising considerably, whereas it has been falling (slightly) in terms of outflows.

Figure 3. U.S. FDI Inflows and Outflows by Country/Region, 2000 and 2012

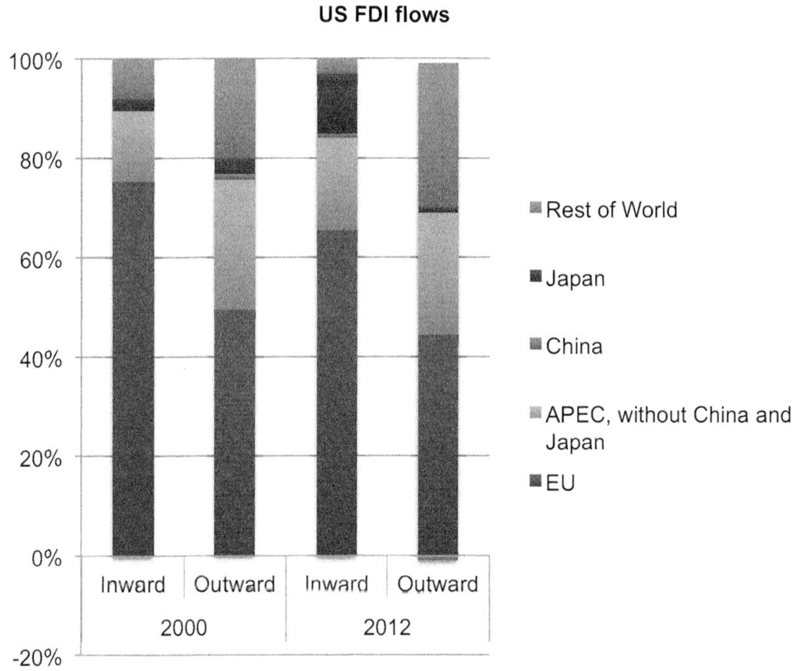

US FDI flows

Source: OECD Stat.

As of 2012, U.S. FDI stocks in the EU were valued at over $2.2 trillion, and EU FDI stocks in the United States were valued at over $1.6 trillion; hence, each economy has a major corporate presence in the other. By sector, the highest concentration of EU FDI in the United States is in manufacturing (36%) as of 2012, with 11% of total stocks being invested in the chemicals sector alone (Figure 5). Investment in finance comprises 14% of total stocks. In recent years, according to Hamilton and Quinlan,[9] European financial firms have been decreasing their U.S. presence yet European companies have been increasing investments in automobile manufacturing and energy. By sector, in 2013, the largest European M&A deals in the United States were in communications and pharmaceuticals.[10] U.S. investment in the EU

---

[9]Daniel S. Hamilton, and Joseph P. Quinlan, *The Transatlantic Economy 2013*. Washington, DC: Center for Transatlantic Relations, 2013.

Figure 4. EU FDI Flows by Country/Region, 2000 and 2013

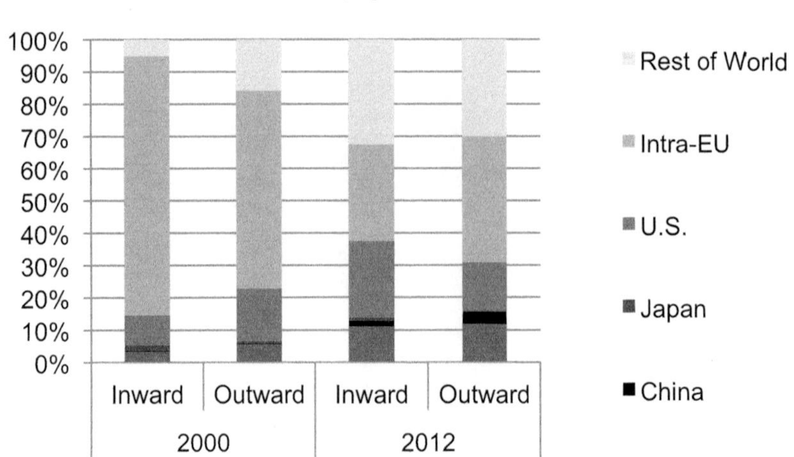

Source: OECD Stat.

has markedly different shares in these sectors. Over half of the 2012 stock of U.S. investment in the EU was in nonbank holding companies, with only 12% in manufacturing sectors.

Economics of the TTIP

It has often been said that the United States and the EU do not need an FTA because they already have very liberal economies and the marginal benefits of the TTIP are not worth the political costs. Better invest, the argument usually goes, in multilateral negotiations or bilateral/regional agreements elsewhere.

It is true that tariff levels between the EU and United States are already fairly low, estimated to be under 4% on average.[11] Though some high tariffs remain, such as tariff rates over 20% in both the EU and the United States on trucks, most of the gains and the challenges are to be found in removing various non-tariff measures (NTMs),

---

[10]Ibid, p. 8.

[11]www.wto.org.

Figure 5. Sectoral Breakdown of U.S. and EU Inward FDI Stocks, 2012

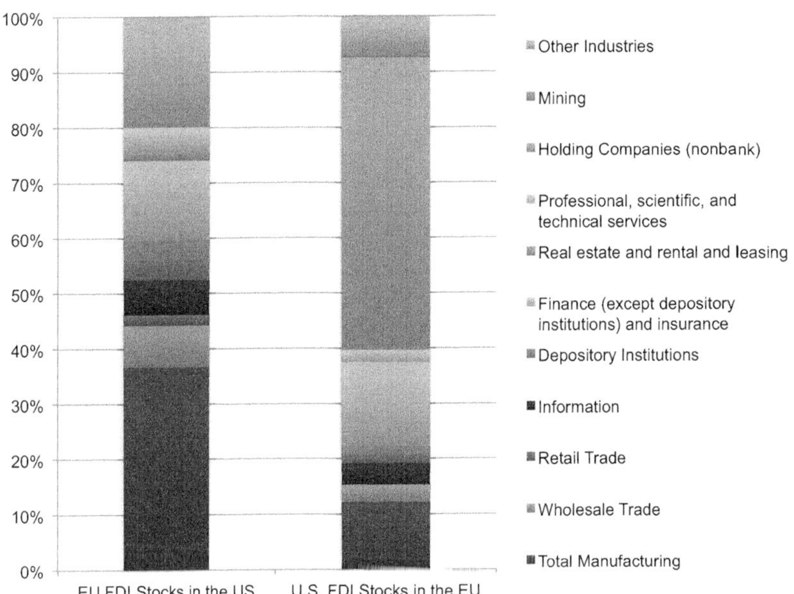

Source: BEA, Balance of Payments and Direct Investment Position Data.

such as the estimated 26% ad valorem tariff equivalent cost that different vehicle requirements between the EU and the United States creates. It has been widely cited that 80% percent of the benefits of TTIP would be generated through the removal of NTMs.[12] Estimating the effects of NTMs is much more of an art than a science, but few would dispute that they are much more significant.

In 2009 Berden et al.[13] estimated trade costs between the EU and the United States to be, on average, approximately 3-4% of total trade

---

[12]American Chamber of Commerce to the European Union, "EU's position on the Transatlantic Trade and Investment Partnership (TTIP): Building the Framework for Strengthening the Transatlantic Partnership," March 14, 2014. Available at: http://tradeinvest.babinc.org/wp-content/uploads/2014/03/AmCham-EU%E2%80%99s-position-on-the-Transatlantic-Trade-and-Investment-Partnersh...-1.pdf.

[13]Koen G. Berden, Joseph Francois, Martin Thelle, Paul Wymenga, and Saara Tamminen. "Non-Tariff Measures in EU-US Trade and Investment – An Economic Analysis," ECORYS, December 11, 2009.

in goods and services ($919 billion). They found that NTMs increased costs for EU and U.S. firms in approximately 60% of cases, as well as creating economic rent in 40% of them. The paper used a Computable General Equilibrium (CGE) model to estimate a standard liberalization scenario in which 50% of current NTMs between the United States and the EU are removed, as well as a more modest scenario of 25% of NTMs. The results were impressive for a relatively-standard CGE model: under the 50% liberalization scenario, the paper estimated an increase in EU GDP of 0.7% in 2018 relative to the baseline, or $158 billion. The commensurate change in U.S. GDP was 0.3% ($53 billion), due in large part to a more open market to start. They also estimated household incomes to increase by up to 0.8% per year in 2018 in the EU and 0.3% in the United States. Wage increases in the EU as a result of productivity gains from removal of NTMs were 0.8% per year in the EU and 0.4% per year in the United States. Changes in exports in the ambitious scenario would be relatively equal in absolute terms, but in terms of shares U.S. exports would increase by 6.1% relative to the baseline and EU exports by 2.1%. The EU gains more than the United States in removals of NTMs in aerospace, automotives, chemicals, cosmetics, and pharmaceuticals. The study identified potential for additional gains in the removal of the U.S. requirement of 100% container scanning ($12.7 billion per year for the EU and the United States combined), decreasing foreign barriers to government procurement ($13.8 billion per year for the EU and United States combined), and convergence of IPR regimes ($1.1 billion per year, for both combined).

These are actually impressive gains for the type of model used, but at an aggregate level, obviously fail to make a strong case for integration. However, in 2005 the OECD estimated potential welfare gains to the EU and the United States could be as high as 3-3.5% of GDP,[14] which is similar to the 2.5-3% Berden et. al. estimated with removal of 100% of NTMs (which is obviously unattainable but limited to NTMs[15]).

---

[14]OECD. "The Transatlantic Trade and Partnership Agreement: Why Does it Matter?" n.d. Accessed March 30, 2014.

[15]Lester and Barbee note that some of the NTMs considered in Berden et al (2009) cannot easily be remedied, and that their ambitious scenario would require tort reform in the United States and addressing the postal monopolies in both the EU and the United States.

Building on these findings, Francois, et al. use responses to survey questions to calculate the degree of non-tariff barriers (NTBs) foreign firms face in the United States and the EU in terms of FDI. This NTB index for FDI is approximately 28 for non-EU firms in the EU and 18 for EU firms within the EU. The U.S. NTB index for FDI is 24.[16] In financial services, construction, insurance, and business services, the EU appears to have relatively equal levels of openness *vis a vis* intra-EU and extra-EU firms. For goods, the most significant partner/non-partner differences lie in aerospace, chemicals (this includes drugs and cosmetics), and motor vehicles.[17] Comparing EU and U.S. openness to FDI by sector, the authors find that both the United States and the EU are relatively open compared to the rest of the world, with the exceptions being in aerospace (both the United States and the EU), motor vehicles (the EU), cosmetics (the EU), ICT (the EU), and transport (the United States).[18]

Their results indicate that a 10% increase in the NTB index (e.g., from 20 to 22) will be accompanied by a 5% reduction in observed income from foreign investment. They estimate that if EU firms faced the same levels of access on the NTB index in the United States as they do in the EU (down to 18 from 24), the resulting gains for affiliates of EU firms would be approximately €10 billion.

While the above review would suggest that TTIP could have an important bearing on certain sectors in the EU and the United States, as noted above, the small aggregate effects on the two economies had led to a great deal of skepticism regarding the need for TTIP. Alan Winters, for example, notes that a "plausible" TTIP would lead to only about a 0.035% increase in GDP for the EU and U.S. economies, and a very ambitious one might lead to an increase of

---

The authors argue that while the regulatory reforms of TTIP are important and beneficial, the effects will likely be less significant. See Simon Lester and Inu Barbee, "Tackling Regulatory Trade Barriers in the Transatlantic Trade and Investment Partnership," Bertelsmann Stiftung: Future Challenges, February 2014, available at: http://futurechallenges.org/local/tackling-regulatory-trade-barriers-in-the-transatlantic-trade-and-investment-partnership/

[16]Joseph Francois, Miriam Manchin, Hanna Norberg, Olga Pindyuk, and Patrick Tomberger. "Reducing Trans-Atlantic Barriers to Trade and Investment," Center for Economic Policy Research, March 2013, p. 86.

[17]Ibid., p. 87.

[18]Ibid., p. 88.

about 0.05%.[19] As these numbers are low, he concludes, better to work at the multilateral level and in integrating China.

While these latter recommendations are no doubt laudable, it is essential to not take the estimates of CGE models too seriously when trying to capture the likely gains from an agreement, as they tend to be seriously downward-biased.[20] For example, in addition to the failure to effectively account for NTMs, other border and behind-the-border trade costs, and firm heterogeneity, these CGEs tend to exclude FDI, which are difficult to incorporate due to data issues, model specifications, and other technical issues (only a few models have been able to do this for any configuration, let alone TTIP). This is a major problem in the context of the TTIP given the importance of transatlantic FDI flows and the extremely large stock of EU and U.S. FDI in other's economic space; one ignores an aggregate sum of $3.8 trillion in FDI (noted above) at her or his own peril.

An example might illustrate the point. Any CGE estimates of gains from the EU Single Market Programme, if the modelling mainly relied on tariff liberalization and NTMs, would have been extremely low, given that there was a customs union in place for twenty years prior and the internal and external NTMs were relatively minor. Realizing this, the Cecchini Report (1988) attempted to give a more realistic view of what the attendant benefits would be by trying to calculate the effects of non-traditional areas, in effect looking at the "costs of non-Europe." The estimates were large (up to more than 5% of EU GDP), and while many economists suggested that certain aspects of the estimates were overly optimistic, few today would argue that the effects of the Single Market have been negligible.

The same may be true of the TTIP. The Cecchini Report was a massive and very expensive study; it is unlikely that there will be any similar initiative in the context of the TTIP. However, the Single Market example does teach us to take with a grain of salt results from models that are not able endogenize or account for key aspects of the initiative.

---

[19]See http://www.voxeu.org/article/problem-ttip.

[20]See, for example, Fan Zhai, "Armington Meets Melitz: Introducing Firm Heterogeneity in a Global CGE Model of Trade," *Journal of Economic Integration*, 23(3), September 2008, pp. 575–604.

In sum, there are strong reasons to believe that TTIP will generate significant transatlantic benefits, even if these gains don't always show up in the formal modelling. As a final point, it is, perhaps, worth noting that in the context of a fairly weak economic recovery in the United States and continued stagnation in the EU, the 3-3.5% increase in GDP estimated in OECD (2005) is actually fairly significant: it constitutes a non-debt-creating stimulus that would not only generate allocative efficiency gains through specialization but also could boost the (dismal) growth perceptions in the EU, which in turn could have a strong effect on investment in the relatively short term. In a region that grew by only 0.1% in 2013 and has actually contracted by 0.3% since 2008, such a positive shock would no doubt be very welcome.[21]

TTIP in a Global Context

Especially over the past quarter century, there has been a global embrace of the international marketplace. This does not mean that all countries have accepted a "neoliberal" world view (whatever that means). Rather, policymakers have recognised the attendant potential benefits of an outward-oriented development strategy. And this includes both non-OECD as well as OECD countries. Indeed, from the 1950s until the 1970s developed countries were the most enthusiastic about international trade and investment and developing countries were reticent.[22] These days the opposite is true. Nevertheless, at G-7, G-8, G-20 and other meetings, it is clear from words and deeds that policymakers of the world's most important economies are seeking ways of achieving deeper integration.

The United States and the EU have always played a critical role in international governance of trade and finance, but the shift in economic gravity toward the South, and particularly Asia, is leading to a good deal of pressure on these institutions, which are struggling to adapt. In terms of trade, the regionalism movement has replaced multilateral approaches to global governance, at least in the short-term. How the

---

[21]EUROSTAT, http://epp.eurostat.ec.europa.eu/tgm/table.do?tab=table&init=1&plugin=1&language=en&pcode=tec00115, accessed June 17, 2014.

[22]Jagdish N. Bhagwati, *Free Trade Today* (Princeton: Princeton University Press, 2002).

United States and the EU should respond to the new associated challenges is an extremely important question, particularly given Asia's deepening embrace of regionalism and its rising global importance.

There are several possible options to meet these new challenges.

The United States has responded by striving to be part of the Asian integration process. This has been true for some time, e.g., as a key player in APEC, its advocacy under the "Enterprise for ASEAN Initiative," its bilateral FTAs (South Korea, Singapore), its new membership in the East Asian Summit, and more recently the TPP and the APEC-relate Free-Trade Area of the Asia-Pacific (FTAAP) proposal, which is slated to begin negotiations in favor of an APEC-wide FTA in 2020 (indeed, the TPP and Asian—now RCEP—"tracks" would ultimately merge into the FTAAP, at least that was the agreement at the 2010 APEC Summit in Yokohama, Japan). But, of course, the United States is a Pacific power; it has had strong strategic interests in the region for a half-century and extensive economic interests in the region for almost as long. The EU is not a Pacific power; its strategic and economic focus has been in Europe—consolidating and expanding the most extensive and complicated economic integration process in the world—and in Africa, as well as North America. It is a member of the Asia-Europe Meeting (ASEM) but, in general, the EU has come late to the regionalism game in Asia. In addition to its 2011 FTA with South Korea, it has gone through a series of negotiations with ASEAN toward a possible FTA (as well as Singapore bilaterally). Should it be more active in developing closer ties with the Asia-Pacific?

The economic literature is somewhat mixed in this regard, but in general the potential economic effects of various EU-Asia accords are not particularly significant, given the relatively liberal environments and low intensity of trade. Perhaps this explains a rather relaxed attitude of EU policymakers with regard to the regionalism movement in Asia. Still, they could have important sectoral effects, particularly in the area of services. Trade in services is one area that has been much neglected at the multilateral level and, hence, it should come as no surprise that gains in this area could be significant.

In any event, pushing hard for a deep, comprehensive Doha Development Agreement (DDA) once it becomes politically possible again would certainly be an effective strategy for the EU. A strong multilateral deal would mitigate any potential trade and investment diversion effects; ensure that commercial governance continues to be global rather than regional; and allow the EU to exert influence via negotiations, particularly in areas it deems to be the most important. The United States also has a strong interest in the ultimate success of the DDA.

But unfortunately there are significant headwinds against a strong DDA. The "Bali Package" worked out at the December 2013 Ministerial may have been a bit of a pyrrhic victory; while ultimately members arrived at a deal (that is still being codified at the time of this writing), the fact that one country, India, was able to hold up the entire agreement (arguably for domestic political reasons) until "overtime," followed by "extra innings" when Cuba held up the meetings for another day, does not bode well for a deep, comprehensive agreement among 159 diverse member-economies. It certainly underscored a certain resistance to deep integration, which has plagued the DDA negotiations from its early years. Modern regionalism is being driven by a need to breakdown real inhibitors to economic integration to facilitate, *inter alia*, the creation of regional production networks. Hence, unlike the case of European economic integration, regionalism especially in Asia is market-driven, i.e., bottom-up rather than top-down. The vector of measures necessary to accomplish market-friendly deep integration is politically difficult particularly in the more liberalization-shy economies, which is why it would be difficult for the DDA to keep up with the needs of the private sector. On the hand, prospects for liberalization of "high hanging fruit" in the context of a smaller set of outward-oriented, "like minded" economies are brighter.

Thus, while continuing to work at the DDA makes a great deal of sense, the "mega-regionalism movement" is picking up steam and will likely continue into the foreseeable future. The TPP has taken longer to finish than its negotiators had hoped; however, the expansion to include Japan in 2013 was sure to slow it down and, given that 2014 is an election year in the United States, only the very brave would anticipate an agreement then. But 2015 is a different story. And a successful TPP will no doubt energize negotiators at RCEP to move forward on a deal.

This is the context in which TTIP is playing out. TTIP is in the interest of both the United States and the EU and, ultimately, the global trading system in general. The reasoning might have less to do with anticipated direct economic benefits that would accrue from such an accord—though these could be large. As discussed above, while the very liberal structure of EU and U.S. trade and investment protection has led some modellers to derive fairly modest effects, the real impact could be much greater—including the indirect benefits of deeper cooperation. In particular, the TTIP could contribute to a strengthening of EU-U.S. leadership at the WTO, which in turn could help them kick-start and lead more effectively at the DDA. It would allow for the United States and the EU to show leadership in creating a modern "gold standard" FTA, which obviously would be easier to do in the case of EU-United States than in the context of the TPP, given the similarities of interest and advanced production processes. For example, services trade, be it cross-border or through commercial presence, is a strong and growing part of the EU-U.S. economic relationship. An EU-U.S. accord could create a template for services, as well as in other areas such as competition policy, intellectual property protection, and the like.

Assuming that the TPP track develops on target, an EU-U.S. FTA would also allow European firms to benefit from the transpacific integration process. We do not know what type of rules of origin requirements will come out of the TPP, but it is likely that cumulation rules will facilitate the development of production networks for European firms. Should this be the case, the EU will have succeeded in reducing significantly the greatest potential source of trade diversion of Asia-Pacific economic cooperation.

Certainly many of the above proposals will be politically difficult. But none of them are really new; they have just lacked sufficient political backing. Recent trends in global commercial policy have shown us that many things previously believed to be politically impossible have all of a sudden become not only feasible but even probable. Hopefully EU and U.S. policymakers will seize upon these emerging opportunities and influence them in such a way as to strengthen the international system and global growth and development.

Chapter 9

CETA and TIIP:
Implications and Lessons Learned

Colin Robertson

Getting it Done

Canadian Prime Minister Stephen Harper and European Commission President José Manuel Barroso announced an agreement in principle on a Comprehensive Economic and Trade Agreement (CETA) on October 18, 2013. The European Commission and Canadian Government have both released explanatory documents, and the final document is also now available. The agreement will remove over 99% of tariffs between the two economies and open new opportunities in services and investment. Once implemented, the agreement is expected to increase two-way bilateral trade in goods and services by 23%. CETA is a forward-looking agreement that includes built-in review. The agreement opens Canadian provincial and municipal procurement estimated at $100 billion and, for Canadians, the $2.7 trillion EU government procurement market.

While the final document has now been negotiated, the October announcement was premature by normal standards and motivated by Canadian domestic political imperatives, including the return of Parliament and the Conservative party policy convention. There was also a sense that EU patience for continued negotiations was at an end. After any last-minute clarifications are made to the final negotiated text, there will be a legal "scrub" and then translation of the document into 24 languages. Based on the EU's bilateral agreements with Colombia, Peru, and South Korea, this step could take up to a year. As a requirement of such a free trade agreement, the Europeans also insist on conclusion of a potentially politically-sensitive Strategic Partnership Agreement on foreign policy and sectoral cooperation.

With the February 2013 State of the Union announcement by President Obama of the EU-U.S. Transatlantic Trade and Investment Partnership (TTIP) negotiations, EU negotiators turned their attention to the new deal. There was a strong risk that the Canadian deal could become stranded. The Canadian business community called on the government for a "rapid and successful conclusion" of a deal most thought could have been done in the spring. Before the agreement comes into force it will need to be approved by the European Council, then the European Parliament, followed by ratification, as appropriate, by member states. European Parliament elections in May 2014 have altered the makeup of its trade committee, which had been a strong supporter of an agreement. On the Canadian side, implementing legislation needs to be passed by both the federal parliament and provincial legislatures. The entire implementation could take 2–3 years, although provisional application of most of the agreement could begin earlier.

The CETA process began in Berlin at the 2007 EU-Canada Summit when leaders agreed to a joint study examining the costs and benefits of a closer economic partnership. After review at the 2008 Canada-EU Summit, a "Scoping Exercise" (Joint Report on the EU-Canada Scoping Exercise) set the parameters for the negotiations that began at the EU-Canada Summit on May 6, 2009 in Prague. The EU subsequently (June, 2011) conducted a Sustainability Impact Assessment (SIA) on the CETA's social, environmental and economic impact. Within Canada, the Standing Committee on International Trade conducted hearings on the proposed agreement in 2011 and released their report in March, 2012 with the Government response following in June, 2012. The committee is currently conducting hearings into the agreement.

The European Union is the world's largest single common market comprising 28 member states, a total population of over 500 million, and a GDP of $17.4 trillion. Canada, a confederation of ten provinces and three territories, has a population of 35 million with a GDP of $1.8 billion. As a bloc, the EU represents Canada's second largest trading partner (after the United States) with around 9.5% of Canada's total external trade. Canada is the EU's twelfth largest trading partner accounting for 1.8% of the EU's total external trade. It is estimated that 375,000 Canadian jobs rely on trade with the EU. European investment in Canada is worth more than $171 billion, representing over 24% of total foreign investment in Canada, while Canadian direct investment in the EU amounted to $181 billion in 2012, representing over 28% of Canadian direct investment abroad.

The top 10 Canadian exports to the EU in 2012 were gold, crude petroleum, diamonds, iron ore, uranium, nickel, aircraft, soya beans, coal and copper. Top ten EU exports were: drugs, luxury cars, light and crude petroleum, wines, medical instruments, motor vehicles, aircraft and machinery parts, and wind generators.

The 2008 joint report predicts that within seven years of implementation annual real income gains will be approximately €11.6 billion for the EU and €8.2 billion for Canada. Canadian exports to the EU are predicted to increase by 20.6% or €8.6 billion while EU exports to Canada are estimated to rise by 24.3% or €17 billion. These figures represent gains resulting from the elimination of tariffs, the liberalization of trade in services, and cost savings from fewer non-tariff barriers. Half of the expected GDP gains for the EU are related to trade in services and a quarter to the removal of tariffs. The remaining 25% will occur with the removal of non-tariff barriers (NTBs) and result in a €2.9 billion gain for the EU and €1.7 billion for Canada. The Canadian Government's CETA Summary says the gains are the economic equivalent of adding $1,000 to the average Canadian family's income and almost 80,000 new jobs to the Canadian economy. The prior arrangements for Canada-EU trade were governed by the GATT/WTO and the 1975 Framework Agreement for Commercial and Economic Cooperation that established annual EU-Canada summits. Subsequent agreements covered customs administration (1997), trade in live animals and animal products (1999), Wine and Spirits Agreement (2003), the Civil Aviation Safety Agreement (2009) and the Comprehensive Air Transport Agreement (2009).

What the Agreement Does[1]

Trade in Goods

Tariff Elimination: When implemented, CETA will ensure that Canada and the EU provide each other's goods with "national treatment" aside from customs duties and other fees allowed by the World

---

[1] This draws heavily from the post-announcement summaries released by the EU - Facts and Figures, and Canadian Agreement Overview. The most detailed summary of this still-to-be-completed agreement can be found in the Canadian Technical Summary of Final Negotiated Outcomes. There is also useful testimony before the Canadian House of Commons Standing Committee on International Trade in its examination of CETA

Trade Organization (WTO). CETA's rules of origin are intended to reflect global value chains and the reality that goods are made from parts or ingredients ("inputs") sourced from many countries.

Duties will be eliminated on 98% of over 9,000 tariff lines. This includes nearly 100% of non-agricultural tariff lines and close to 94% of agricultural tariff lines. Once CETA is fully implemented, approximately 99% of the EU's tariff lines will be duty-free, including 100% of more than 7,000 non-agricultural tariff lines and over 95% of more than 1,900 agriculture tariff lines. Another 1% of tariffs will be eliminated over a period of up to seven years.

The EU reckons it will save exporters around €500 million in industrial duties annually, and sees new opportunities especially in consumer goods, e.g. the upper end of the clothing market and items like perfume. By the end of the transitional periods, Canada and the EU will liberalize, respectively, 92.8% and 93.5% of trade lines in agriculture.

Tariffs phased-out by the EU include those on some fish and seafood products, grains and passenger vehicles. This includes transitional tariff rate quotas (TRQs) for key Canadian exports (23,000 tons of shrimp and 1,000 tons of cod). Canadians also see new opportunities on exports of minerals (e.g. aluminum, nickel). Canadian tariffs that will be phased-out include those on passenger vehicles (three, five and seven years), certain agricultural goods (three, five and seven years) and ships (three and seven years).

Canadian dairy products and EU beef, pork and sweet corn will get tariff rate quota access increases amounting to a further 1% and 1.9% of tariff lines respectively. There are gains for Canadian beef and pork producers. Canadian consumers should get both more choice and a better price on with the bigger quota for EU cheese (an additional 4% access after phase-in). Canadian tariffs on EU prepared agricultural products (PAPs), notably wine (EU provides half of Canadian wine imports) will be eliminated as will other relevant trade barriers.

Besides eliminating tariffs, the EU processing industry will gain better access to Canadian fish. Sustainable fisheries, with commitment to monitoring, control and surveillance measures, will be developed.

Non-Tariff Barriers (NTBs): CETA builds on existing rules contained in the WTO Agreement on Technical Barriers to Trade (TBT). The TBT chapter commits to recognition of equivalency and conformity assessment (including marking and labeling provisions) by standard-setting bodies. As appropriate, interested persons in either Canada or the EU will be able to participate in TBT-setting exercises. This should reduce the cost of complying with technical regulations. The EU reckons this will give it GDP gains of up to €2.9 billion.

Regulatory Cooperation: CETA is the first bilateral trade agreement in which Canada has included provisions on regulatory cooperation. Canada and the EU will identify joint cooperative activities and establish an annual high-level dialogue on regulatory matters.

Automotive Sector: Canada will recognize a list of EU car standards and look positively to future standards. CETA interpretation of rules of origin should allow 100,000 of Canada's NAFTA-mobiles (cars assembled in Canada with U.S. and Mexican parts) to be accepted duty-free in the EU every year.

Sanitary and Phytosanitary (SPS): The existing Veterinary Agreement is updated. A new SPS Measures Joint Management Committee provides a venue for experts to discuss issues before they become major problems and to determine which Canadian and EU inspection standards and certification systems both parties can accept as being equivalent to their own. Decisions are to be made based on science. This is especially important for Canada's grain industry. In 2012, Canada had the fourth-largest area planted to biotech crops worldwide, with 97.5% of Canadian-grown canola planted with biotech varieties.

Subsidies: Canada and the EU have agreed to comply with WTO disciplines on subsidies, except in the case of agricultural export subsidies on bilateral trade that are prohibited for all agricultural products where tariffs are eliminated (thus precluding EU export subsidies in Canada-U.S. trade for wheat and coarse grains). Both accept WTO obligations to be transparent and to accept consultations on subsidy programs.

Trade Remedies: CETA reflects WTO rules requiring fair and transparent investigation to determine whether unfair trade is taking place before the country imposes a trade remedy.

Investment, Services and Other Matters

Trade in services: Accounting for over 70% of Canada's GDP, the services sector is by far the largest part of Canada's economy. This is equally important to the EU. Expanded trade in services in key sectors such as financial services, telecommunications, energy and maritime transport will provide half of the EU's overall GDP gains (with potential annual gains of up to €5.8 billion). As in all of its free trade agreements, Canada has excluded key services including health care, public education and other social services.

Temporary movement of company personnel: CETA's temporary-entry provisions will expand on existing WTO access, making it easier to temporarily move staff between the EU and Canada. A framework will facilitate temporary travel or relocation for selected categories of business persons (managers, professionals and trainees), including short-term business visitors, investors, intra-company transferees, and professionals and technologists. Certain professional categories (e.g. engineering, accounting, architecture) will have easier access to temporarily supply consulting services and after-sales maintenance and monitoring commitments.

Mutual recognition of qualifications: CETA looks to future mutual recognition of qualifications in professions including architects, engineers, foresters and accountants. CETA is the first Canadian free trade agreement to include substantive and binding provisions on the mutual recognition of professional qualifications. Under NAFTA there were a host of working groups. If business is wise and active, the provisions in CETA provide an opportunity to assess conformity of Canadian products with EU technical regulations and streamline.

Investment: Combined EU and Canadian FDI stocks amounted to €360 billion in 2011. CETA will remove or alleviate barriers to investment horizontally and in specific sectors. There is an investor-to-state dispute settlement (ISDS) mechanism with protections against abuse and frivolous claims. This includes an independent arbitration panel hearing facts and making a decision on the merits of an investor's claim with the participation of non-disputing parties.

ISDS rules have been a standard feature of Canada's comprehensive free trade agreements since the North American Free Trade Agreement. CETA protects the *Investment Canada Act* (ICA) and the government's right to conduct reviews of high-value investments to ensure that they are of net benefit to Canada. Ministerial decisions on whether or not to permit investments under the ICA, including for national security reasons, are not subject to CETA dispute settlement.

There are two types of reservations for services and investment provisions: Annex II reservations provide complete policy flexibility; Annex I reservations mean that any unilateral liberalization made over a period of time would be captured and locked in at that new level of liberalization.

The special investment rules for the EU, allowing for an increased review threshold under the Investment Canada Act, should also extend to investors from other countries with which Canada has trade agreements with investment protection provisions i.e. the United States and Mexico under NAFTA, but also Colombia, Peru, Chile and Panama. There is a potential opening up of investment flows as a result.

Competition: CETA includes provisions recognizing that Canada and the EU are free to enforce their respective domestic competition legislation. CETA includes rules for monopolies and state enterprises.

Public procurement: All federal and sub-federal levels of government in Canada and the EU will open their procurement markets. Procurement thresholds for Canada in the EU are the same as domestic procurement directive; Canada gets the same level of access as EU member states give to each other in almost every aspect. In Canada, the EU gets access for high value contracts as with Canada-U.S. agreements (through FTA/NAFTA and similar to the 2010 reciprocity agreement at the state-province level under the WTO General Agreement on Agreement GPA).

There are exceptions for cultural industries, aboriginal businesses, defense, research and development, financial services, services in the fields of recreation, sport and education, Canadian airport authorities and Canada Port Authorities, as well as social and health-care services. Rolling stock retains a 25% Canadian content value. There are also specific regional economic development exclusions for Manitoba, Newfoundland and Labrador, Nova Scotia, Northwest Territories, Nunavut, Prince Edward Island, New Brunswick and Yukon. There is full flexibility to specify environmental and social criteria and to have relevant experience as part of the requirement for the tender, which would tend to favor local operations.

CETA applies only to high-value procurement contracts. Governments can continue to use procurement to support local development, especially small and medium-sized enterprises. The threshold-value for procurement contracts in CETA will range from 130,000 to five million special drawing rights (an international value of the International Monetary Fund for which the corresponding range is $205,000 to $7.8 million for the 2012-2013 biannual cycle). This is comparable with Canada's thresholds in the WTO and well above the value set under Canada's Agreement on Internal Trade, which starts at $25,000.

The EU-Canada Joint Study (2008) estimated that Canada's federal government awarded contracts worth 15 to 19 billion Canadian dollars per year. Procurements by Canadian municipalities in 2011 were estimated at 112 billion Canadian dollars (approx. €82 billion) or almost 7% of Canadian GDP. Canada will also create a single electronic procurement website combining information on all tenders and access to public procurement at all levels of government.

Intellectual Property Rights (IPR): CETA will create more of a level playing field between Canada and the EU through complementary but separate approaches. Specifically: patent term restoration (no more than two years for Canada vs. five for the EU), extended data exclusivity (to eight years in Canada versus ten in the EU), and right of appeal for brand-name drug manufacturers in the CETA (details still to be unveiled). There is a renewed commitment to combatting counterfeit goods.

The agreement strengthens the Canadian IPR system in pharmaceuticals through extended protection. Canada is not a big player in the global pharmaceutical market (with 2.6% market share). About 85% of the drugs consumed in Canada are imports, either from the United States or the European Union. About half of Canadian production is exported, mostly to United States.

Copyright: CETA brings Canada in line with World Intellectual Property Organization Treaties on Copyright, and Performances and Phonograms.

Trademarks and Designs: Canada did not take on any commitments in this area but agreed to make reasonable efforts to comply with the Singapore Treaty on the Law of Trademarks, the Protocol Related to the Madrid Agreement Concerning the International Registration of Marks, and the Geneva Act of the Hague Agreement Concerning the International Registration of Industrial Designs.

Geographical Indications (GIs): CETA extends guaranteed name-protection (e.g. French Cognac and Canadian Whisky) to products with names like Grana Padano, Roquefort, Elia Kalamatas Olives, Aceto balsamico di Modena and Chabichou du Poitou. Prosciutto di Parma and Prosciutto di San Daniele can now use their names in Canada. Enforcement of GIs in the Canadian market remains a private matter to be argued before the courts.

Domestic Regulations: Included for the first time in a Canadian agreement, Canada and the EU will base their domestic licensing and qualification decisions on simple, clear, publicly available, reasonable and impartial criteria.

Telecommunications: CETA gives domestic players in the telecommunications market fair access to networks and services, and ensures that regulators act impartially, objectively and in a transparent manner.

Financial Services: Recognizing the role that banks, insurance companies and other financial institutions play in the economy, CETA includes provisions that safeguard the government's right to take prudential measures to protect the stability and integrity of the financial system. Disputes will be addressed using CETA's special dispute settlement rules for financial services.

Sustainable Development

CETA commits to sustainable investment and trade relations respecting environmental, social and labor rights. The Trade and Sustainable Development chapter will create mechanisms for EU and Canadian civil society involvement in the implementation and monitoring of CETA. A dedicated arbitration mechanism, including government consultations and a panel of experts will be established.

Forums for discussion in areas including forestry, fisheries, aquaculture, biotechnology and raw materials are established, with emphasis on science-based approval processes. CETA includes a commitment to cooperate in international forums dealing with issues relevant for both trade and environmental policies, including the WTO, the Organization for Economic Co-operation and Development, and the United Nations Environment Programme.

Dispute Settlement Mechanism Including Mediation

Negotiators drew on lessons learned from the NAFTA and Canada-U.S. softwood lumber disputes, as well as the investor-state challenges under NAFTA Chapter XI. They were determined to make the process more transparent but to preserve and defend governments' ability to regulate. CETA contains a streamlined horizontal mechanism, that includes a fixed set of procedures and time-frames, and covers most areas of CETA. Should formal consultations fail, there is provision for an arbitration panel of independent legal experts drawing from a roster of specialized experts. CETA includes a more robust voluntary mediation mechanism than has been included in Canada's previous trade agreements. CETA includes exceptions, as do all of Canada's free trade agreements, for measures including environmental protection, cultural industries, taxation, and balance of payments.

Looking Forward

CETA creates a framework for business engagement, such as compatibility and equivalency of regulation.

Implications for Canada

By opening new opportunities, trade agreements have the potential to change attitudes. Trade liberalization is as much about developing new norms of behavior as well as adhering to new rules and regulations. If opportunities are realized, CETA should boost gross domestic product, stimulate the creation of more jobs, reduce costs for taxpayers in Canada, promote two-way investment flows and help Canadian enterprise gain in the European market. Specifically CETA will:

- support and advance the strategic goal, endorsed by the provinces and business, of diversifying Canada's international trade and commercial relations. Over time Canada would be less dependent on the United States.

- expand and promote trade in services between Canada and the EU. These will include engineering, professional, computer and information, and scientific and technical services.

- open-up government procurement markets both in the EU and in Canada. The EU procurement market is worth almost $3 trillion a year.

- encourage greater direct foreign investment between Canada and the EU, and strengthen investor protection.

- better position Canada in the Trans-Pacific Partnership and WTO because it raises the bar in agricultural products, intellectual property, foreign investment, and services.

The EU is collectively the largest marketplace and economy in the world, accounting for about a fifth of global economic output, consumption, and production.

Canada currently has a trade deficit with the EU. It also has a qualitative problem in value-added products. CETA opens the potential for a better balance. Canada's top exports are resources: gold, diamonds, iron ore, uranium, petroleum products, wheat, coal, and solid fuels. Amongst the top ten EU exports are medications, motor vehicles, turbo jets and turbines, aerospace parts, wines, biological preparations, machinery parts, and medical instruments.

CETA will move both Canada and the European Union into closer cooperation in many areas of domestic and international regulation. It eliminates tariffs in fisheries, forestry, automotive products, and aluminum—all sectors that Canada has sought to achieve for years. There will be at least a $1 billion increase in pork and beef exports, and it will open up government procurement on both sides. It contains many innovative elements and improvements over previous practices. It creates a bridge—albeit with different paths, different structures, different approaches to individual chapters—between what the European Union did internally with its 28 countries and what Canada, the United States and Mexico did in terms of the North American market.

CETA opens new doors for business services—insurance, finance, engineering, architecture. The average agriculture tariffs to the EU are currently in the 13% to 14% range. These will gradually come down, opening new markets for Canadian grains and, with increased quota, our meat products. That CETA did not begin the phase-out of supply management for dairy and poultry products in Canada is a missed opportunity that means continuing higher cost for Canadian consumers. It makes Canada a less attractive place for value-added food-processing industrial activity.

Trade and investment are the linchpin of the Harper Government's economic growth policy ie. Global Markets Action Plan. Since its election in 2006 it have signed trade agreements with nine countries—Colombia, Jordan, Panama, Peru, the European Free Trade Association (Iceland, Liechtenstein, Norway and Switzerland) and Honduras and reached agreements-in-principle with the 28-country European Union and with Korea.

The search for new markets is motivated by the combination of pull and push. The pull comes from rapidly growing market opportunities in the rest of the world, especially Asia. The push comes from the continuing effect of U.S. political actions hampering market access. The Canada-U.S. FTA and NAFTA created preferred access to the United States but it has been hampered by the security imposed by the United States after 9/11. Initiatives designed to create perimeter security thus allowing better border flow in goods and people and regulatory symmetry are underway but progress is slow and even with safeguards there is always the threat of U.S. protectionism.

Recent events have not been encouraging: the long saga surrounding the Keystone XL pipeline presidential permit; country-of-origin labeling requirements that upset century-old trade in meat; failure to fund the Detroit-Windsor customs plaza; the uncertainties created by sequestration and gridlock in Washington.

The gravitational pull of the U.S. market is powerful. The United States will always be number one for Canada, but the experience of the past five years has heightened the importance of diversification, of building markets overseas. Canada needs to have more trading partners with heft, alternative markets to the United States. Canadians also need to work with others to keep pressure on the United States, at every level of their government and their private sector, to make it in their interest to preserve the liberal trading regime that the USA has much to create.

Always a trading nation, Canada since the FTA/NAFTA has become a nation of traders. The Canadian advantage begins with vast land and bountiful resources. Canada possesses an educated multi-cultural population. Half the population of Toronto, the biggest city in Canada and now fourth largest in North America, was born beyond Canadian borders. Half of Canada's inward migration since 1980 has come from Asia. Canada has a good, if incomplete, logistics system (it needs oil and gas pipelines, more rail capacity and supporting infrastructure at its tidewater ports). Globalization for Canada means defining the country's niche through development of "trade in tasks"within complex international production and supply chain networks that service as many different markets as possible. Export-oriented industries, industries involved in international commerce, whether on the trade or investment side, tend to pay their workers more, tend to have higher productivity, tend to be more innovative.

As to next steps: The Chamber of Commerce and other business groups have argued that Canada needs to step up its public advocacy efforts. A senior level delegation of cabinet ministers, parliamentarians, business and civil society (think tanks, NGOs et al) should meet with key players involved in the European ratification process. It will be especially important to meet new members that may be elected in the May EU parliamentary elections.

Canada needs a network of trained, on-the-ground trade commissioners in all the major countries in Europe. A good trade commissioner service is a tactical leverage point to accelerate time to market in these markets. It needs to be extended. Canada also needs to make more strategic use of trade assets that are already in place. For example, the Export Development Corporation is regularly negotiating pull-lending facilities with major multinationals around the world. The intent of the debt facility is to provide dollar-for-dollar access to Canadian markets and Canadian companies. As economist Jock Finlayson argues, now Canada need to drive to the next level to get access for its companies. With incremental effort at follow-through, Canada can see huge economic benefits to its companies doing trade in these marketplaces. There is also work to do in Canada. The business community needs to develop broader strategies to take advantage of the new market opportunities

A competitive Canada in global markets obliges a competitive market inside Canada. Yet, it is often more difficult to do business between provinces than internationally. Efforts to liberalize internal trade were to match the progress made during the Canada-U.S. FTA. There has been some progress, especially between the western provinces, but nationally it is an unfinished chapter. The Trade Commissioner Service needs to work with the provinces and business associations to encourage more small and medium enterprises to look beyond the United States towards markets internationally. Preparation begins with three questions:

- Do they have the management capacity?

- Do they have the access to capital?

- Do they have the knowledge and information needed to do business?

Implications for North America

When NAFTA was negotiated in 1993–94, there was an expectation that the continental trade pact would be the first step to a free trade pact of the Americas. Ronald Reagan said he "dreamed of a common market stretching from the Yukon to the Yucatan." George H.W. Bush foresaw the day when the countries of North, Central and South America would all be "coequal partners in a free trade zone stretching from the port of Anchorage to Tierra del Fuego." Unfortunately, the Free Trade Agreement of the Americas launched by Bill Clinton at the Miami Summit of the Americas in December, 1994 sputtered out.

After negotiation of the NAFTA there was some expectation that Canada, Mexico and the United States would negotiate future trade agreements as a bloc with other nations, notably Chile, and grow NAFTA. But there was little appetite on the part of any of the partners and the leaders' summits, when held, have effectively been dual bilaterals between the United States and Mexico and the United States and Canada. Each partner subsequently embarked on their own bilateral trade agreements. Mexico was especially active; it now has a network of 11 Free Trade Agreements covering 43 countries, including with the EU.

The Trans-Pacific Partnership negotiations provide an opportunity for NAFTA's revival and renewal. The trilateral summit held in Mexico City in February 2014 heralded the return to regular leaders' meetings (Canada will host in 2015) but the kind of coordinated, collaborative renewal-agenda that would take NAFTA to the next level is not yet evident.

CETA is the first agreement that the EU has with a G-7 country. It is likely that the CETA will be the template for the EU negotiating team (essentially the same group that did the CETA) in the TTIP and this should ensure a degree of symmetry in any deal. According to the Canadian Chief Negotiator, as they negotiated the final stages of the agreement, Canada made a number of connections or linkages to a potential outcome between the United States and the EU, so if the United States and the EU reach an agreement, certain things will be triggered in CETA that will provide Canada with greater benefits.

The United States and the EU are going to face significant obstacles—on agriculture and procurement, for example—to complete an agreement, but the Canada-EU CETA illustrates what can be done. North America's integrated supply chains require access to the EU and the completion of an ambitious, comprehensive TTIP agreement will serve continental interests. In the interim, Canada, the United States and Mexico need to consult with a goal of securing a NAFTA-EU agreement. CETA will not discriminate against USA and Mexican investors because of they are protected through NAFTA. In a commentary for the CD Howe Institute, Lawrence Herman writes that the raising of the threshold for investment review under the *Investment Canada Act* from the current enterprise value level of $344 million to $1.5 billion "will apply equally to investors from the US and Mexico as it does to investors from the European Union." According to Herman, "The North American Free Trade Agreement does not expressly restrict application of the Most-Favored Nation rule with respect to investments, so the rule applies. Investors from the United States and Mexico must be treated on an equal footing and receive the same preferences as EU investors or investments under CETA; like-wise, our other partners in FTAs, such as Peru, Chile and Columbia."

Implications for TTIP

Neither history nor trade negotiations repeat themselves, but inevitably there will be some rhyme to both CETA and TTIP, beginning with the fact that the EU team that will conduct the negotiations is essentially the same group that concluded the Canada-Europe deal. The mindset on the EU side and their starting approach to the outline of the agreement will reflect the Canadian experience. One of the biggest challenges at the outset was to reconcile the EU Single Market approach with the Canada's (arguably North America's) more market-oriented approach of reconciling business interests within the negotiations. Constitutional division of powers obliged the Canadian negotiators to assure that the Canadian provincial representatives were integrated into the negotiations. Managing the U.S. states will not be the same challenge for U.S. negotiators. Canada will be watching TTIP negotiations closely, as CETA is designed to include special "hooks" that will allow the two transatlantic deals to be linked, particularly regarding issues such as standards and rules of origin.

Some specific areas of interest to U.S. TTIP negotiators will include:

- Investor-state provisions have been controversial, especially since being included in the NAFTA agreement, when it was originally intended to give Canadian and U.S. investors greater comfort to invest in Mexico. Instead, such provisions have been applied more often against Canada, at some cost. *The Globe and Mail's* Barrie McKenna reflected popular perception when he wrote that "companies are cleverly stretching the bounds of what they consider an investment" and that "Chapter 11 has become a way for companies either to bypass domestic courts and regulatory agencies, or to get restitution denied through normal channels." Yet the reality, as the Canadian Council of Chief Executive's Vice President, Ailish Campbell, blogged is that "while lawyers may be stretching the boundaries of their attempted applications of NAFTA Chapter

11, the outcomes tell a different story." Judgments have been narrow in scope and Chapter 11 does not limit the government's right to regulate in the public interest. Given the Canadian experience the final agreement is likely to be explicit about the primacy of government. In CETA, negotiators decided to strike a balance, by attempting to provide more protection for governments' right to regulate while simultaneously creating a positive environment for investment.

- *Public procurement.* Thirteen U.S. states have exempted themselves from international agreements, notably the WTO Government Procurement Agreement. Canadian provinces had taken a similar approach, exempting their procurement from the NAFTA, but found with the passage of the U.S. stimulus package that their companies were excluded from bidding. This led to the negotiation (February, 2010) of a reciprocal state-province procurement agreement (albeit with notable exemptions). This issue should not hamper U.S. negotiators given that Canadian provinces obtained wide exemptions from EU procurement.

- *Exemptions.* The U.S. Commerce clause will give USTR negotiators much wider scope for negotiation than their Canadian federal counterparts, who are more constitutionally constrained because of powers explicitly reserved to the provinces. Nonetheless, they must deal with Congress. This should result in a reasonably clear sense of what is not on the table. Assuming the USA and EU take the "negative list" approach it should make it easier to discipline the exemptions. Nonetheless, negotiators should anticipate efforts to discredit the "negative list" approach because of its so-called ratcheting effect, leading to a race to the bottom. There is no evidence to support this and, in the case of investment liberalization, an OECD study observes that NAFTA-inspired agreements, of which the CETA is arguably derivative, "tend to have an advantage in terms of the number of sectors covered by non-discrimination disciplines and the degree of transparency and predictability through a "one-shot" liberalisation encompassing all sectors and a "ratchet" mechanism that locks in future reforms."

- *Agriculture.* This is probably one of the least ambitious chapters, given the preservation of supply management in Canada. This chapter came down to hard negotiations between Canadian negotiators who wanted better access for pork and beef products and the EU wanted better access for dairy products, especially for its cheese.

- *Standards.* The EU is conducting its own consultations on ambition for scope of regulatory provisions. Medical devices, construction products, and consumer products are some of Canada's priorities for common standards. This will need to be an on-going discussion to make it work, and it is something that should eventually embrace North America (including Mexico) and the EU.

- *Rules of Origin.* Canada has a high degree of U.S. inputs into what it produces and ships. CETA includes provision for certification to EU standards in Canada. The EU and the United States may go further than CETA on regulatory standards in TTIP, and this would be a good thing. If we can do this across the board we can assess North American, not just Canadian, content. We need to avoid the spaghetti bowl of growing and differing rules of origin.

- *Energy.* Canada wanted access to the EU market, and the EU is keen to find alternatives to the Middle East and Russia as its own supplies draw down (mindful that the fracking revolution when embraced by Europeans could change this). The challenge for Canada is to build a pipeline to tidewater with accompanying LNG terminals before the U.S. revolution turns it into an energy exporter. Recent events in the Ukraine, notably the Crimean gobble by the Russians, have made a new case for European strategic alternative gas supplies to Russia and Gazprom.

CETA's Lessons

1. The Road to Europe Starts with its National Leaders

In the months leading to the formal decision by the EU to commence free trade negotiations with Canada, Canadian political leadership worked their counterparts in the lead member states. These included discussions between Prime Minister Harper and Nicolas Sarkozy, Angela Merkel and David Cameron. While Canadian governments have sought closer relations with the EU for fifty years, the impetus for the CETA began in 2006 with conversations between Quebec Premier Jean Charest, EU Trade Commissioner Peter Mandelson and French President Nicolas Sarkozy. The Canada-Europe Roundtable led by former Canadian trade minister Roy McLaren provided ongoing encouragement and support. Sarkozy, arguably the most pro-North American French leader since World War II, saw this as the logical first step to a larger agreement between the EU and the United States.

France's interests in Canada were once focused on Quebec; cultural ties with its former colony that were notoriously re-kindled by Charles de Gaulle in 1967 with his "Vive le Quebec libre" speech. Relations with the Canadian government improved under Presidents Mitterrand and Chirac and flourished under President Sarkozy. French investment and trade with the rest of Canada (oil and gas through Total in Alberta and uranium through Arriva in Saskatchewan) are now greater than that with Quebec. Dutch, British, German and other European investment has also increased—after the United States and Switzerland, Canada was the main destination point before it was overtaken by Brazil - and European business support became another argument in favor of a closer relationship.

2. *The Place to Close a Deal is in Brussels*

During the end game, frustrated by the opaque and complicated structure of EU decision-making, Canadian leadership sought to close to close the deal by working through their counterparts in the UK, Germany and France. Ultimately, Prime Minister Harper engaged his counterparts—David Cameron, Angela Merkel and Francois Hollande—both bilaterally and in multilateral forums (G8 and G20). The European leaders individually and collectively advised him to go through the appropriate EU officials—European Commission President José Manuel Barroso and Trade Commissioner Karel de Gucht. The October 2013 announcement spurred negotiators to get the deal done.

3. National Governments Can Lead but Contemporary Trade Deals Require Formal Participation from Sub-National Governments

At the outset the Europeans studied the Canadian constitution and realized that to make the gains they wanted in procurement, services and investment (especially around resources) provincial governments had to be at the table and they must be able to commit municipal governments. As a result of this requirement, Europeans would joke that when the Canadian delegation (initially 120 including provincial representatives) travelled to Brussels they would take an Airbus while the EU delegation could travel in a Bombardier Challenger.

4. Public Eeducation is Necessary on "Why Trade?"

The public is skeptical about trade. Deference to what is widely perceived as closed negotiations by the elite has given way to defiance and populist opposition to new trade deals. This despite the fact that globalization, stimulated by freer trade, has lifted millions from poverty and the percentage of people in the world living on $1 a day has declined by 80% percent since 1970s.

Canada is an outlier in that most Canadians think trade deals work to their advantage, although they, like publics in the United States and EU, increasingly expect attention to social license, environmental and labor issues.

Opposition in Canada came from the Left, labor and environmentalists, with the Council of Canadians leading a campaign on the slogan "Trade with Europe but not at any cost." They focused their opposition around the following:

- drug prices would rise significantly;

- investor-state rights would lead to privatization of Canadian water supplies leading to mass water exports; dairy and cheese producers complained about destruction of their industry;

- municipalities would have to open their procurement to the detriment of "local" contractors.

While the critics found space on editorial pages and succeeded in convincing some city councils and school boards to pass anti-CETA resolutions, the opposition did not find sufficient traction to halt the negotiations.

Political leadership must make the case for trade by identifying these jobs—by factory and company, by county and district, by state. In the case of trade, all politics is truly local. The case for trade has not changed since Adam Smith—trade creates growth and prosperity.

5. Create Structures for Trade Advice

Given its politics and high public visibility, the Canada-U.S. Free Trade Agreement necessitated the creation of a mechanism for provincial, business, labor and civil society input. During the Canada-U.S. Free Trade negotiations the Canadian Government created an International Trade Advisory Committee (ITAC) that involved high-level representation from business with a series of Sectoral Advisory groups (SAGIT) including representation from labor and civil society.

This structure served successive governments through subsequent trade negotiations (NAFTA, GATT/WTO, bilateral agreements) as valuable sources of advice and a sounding board. It developed champions, non-government counterweights to the anti-trade interest groups claiming the process was anti-democratic. No similar body existed during the CETA negotiations, nor was there much effort at an ongoing public information campaign.

To sustain public support and ensure that the agreements have relevance to those who will use them, governments need to actively solicit business engagement. The chief negotiators and lead cabinet ministers need to regularly provide updates and share information.

6. Business Must Be Present and Help Drive the Process

The Canadian business community wanted this deal and their pressure helped keep the political level focused. When it appeared the negotiations might wither away, both individual companies and the various business organizations, both sectoral and aggregate (including the Canadian Council of Chief Executives, Canadian Chamber of Commerce, Canadian Manufacturers and Exporter, Canadian Federation of Independent Business) coalesced to underline their concern both publicly and in private conversations.

7. *Start with a Negative List*

Negotiators agreed to liberalize everything except those sectors specifically exempted. Instead of putting on the table that which both sides were willing to liberalize they had to identify that which is excluded. This obliges special interests to justify their exemption or exclusion.

8. *Keep Other Baggage on a Separate Track*

As with any bilateral relationship there are irritants—trade and political—that aggravate and frustrate relations. At the outset, negotiators agreed to keep these issues—for example, the EU fuel quality directive that threatens the export of oil sands product—on a separate track. Otherwise, these issues will interfere and upset the negotiating process.

9. *Patience*

Trade negotiations take more time than anticipated. Much of that time, especially in negotiations between federations, is spent in developing internal cohesion and agreement on a consolidated series of "asks."

Differences between the various EU secretariats were mirrored by differences between Canadian officials and inter-governmental divisions at the federal as well as provincial levels of government. This complicated the negotiations throughout.

Negotiators spent the first year and a half of the nearly four years explaining the differences between the two sides (and to themselves, given the differences between provincial governments). As Pierre-Marc Johnson, the former Quebec premier and advisor to the Quebec Government observed, "It needed lots of exchange so that on both sides the leads and those under the leads at the different tables understood pretty well the policy making principles behind the words we were using."

10. Sell the Deal Regionally and by Industry Sector

When the deal was announced it received the endorsement in principle of most editorialists and pundits, as well as every provincial premier, and all three of the territorial leaders. This effectively ensured that the agreement was seen as a positive development and reflected as such in the media cycle in the first 24–48 hours after the announcement. The Government conducted a cross-country "selling" effort involving regional ministers making the case for CETA in their region and city and identifying the potential job and investment gains by sector. Four in five Canadians backed the agreement, according to a poll taken in the wake of the deal.

11. Follow-Up is Everything

An agreement opens the door but it is then up to business to make use of the new access. Agreements give opportunity but then business must act to invest and trade.

This approach worked well with the Canada-U.S. FTA and NAFTA, both in terms of outward investment and trade. CETA gives Canada a "first-in" advantage—perhaps 10–15% over the United States in the estimate of Canadian Chief Negotiator Steve Verheul. This can affect investor decisions, especially for value-chain processing within North America and in forming customer relationships.

Government can expedite and facilitate opportunities and put in place framework policies, trade agreements, market access arrangements, and support infrastructure like the trade commissioner service. This is especially important in in a country where most companies are under 100 employees.

Ultimately it is up to companies and entrepreneurs to take advantage of opportunities. Having industry sector associations actively beating the drum and organizing trade missions helps. The Canadian Agri-Food Trade Alliance, for example, expects to expand exports to the EU by $1.5 billion a year (which would be a 63% increase). In parliamentary testimony, the Fisheries Council of Canada called it a "game-changer" for Atlantic Canada's shrimp sector, particularly cooked and peeled shrimp; lobster processing; herring and mackerel sector and a positive impact on the British Columbia groundfish and salmon sectors, and the Northwest Territories and prairie walleye and pickerel sectors.

Chapter 10

The Impact of TTIP on Brazil

Vera Thorstensen and Lucas Ferraz[1]

The world is facing a significant transformation process supported by new paradigms: revolutionary innovations in all fronts, new information technologies, huge and speedy mobility of capital, invention of risky financial tools, and globalization of production. The impact of these phenomena on trade and trade activities is strong and drastic, leaving not much time for the postponement of decisions.

The trading system is facing serious challenges caused by these transformations: difficulty in concluding the 15-year-old multilateral negotiation at the World Trade Organization (WTO); the multiplication of preferential trade agreements (PTAs); and the necessity to reinvent trade rules used to support global value chains.

Given the difficulties encountered in the Doha Round to adapt old trade rules to new realities, the United States and the European Union (EU) decided to launch a new profile of PTAs, including mega-regional trade agreements such as the TTIP (Transatlantic Trade and Investment Partnership) and the TPP (Trans-Pacific Partnership), encompassing half of world trade.

More than the reduction of tariffs, these mega-agreements aim to define a new structure and new modalities for all kinds of non-tariff barriers to trade, along with new rules for important trade-related issues such as investment and competition, and new concerns as environment, climate, labor, food scarcity, animal welfare, privacy standards and mounting consumer pressure.

Brazil, as a global but relatively small international trader, has opted for giving priority to the multilateral track, where it assumed it could influence the game and better defend its interests. However, the conclusion of the Doha Round is more difficult to achieve than expected.

---

[1] The authors would like to thank their research team members Carolina Müller, Rodolfo Cabral, Belisa Eleoterio, and Thiago Nogueira.

Moreover, most countries have chosen another path: to increase their trade through negotiations of PTAs. On the one hand, this strategy creates new market opportunities. On the other hand, it results in the fragmentation of international trade regulation, creating conflicts and lack of transparency.

Nonetheless, this new reality must be confronted. The EU is changing its priorities from the WTO and smaller PTAs and has opted for a new challenge—a negotiation with its most controversial trade partner, the United States. The creation of the TTIP is a revolutionary initiative for the trading system. It will surely benefit the two parties to the negotiation. But at the same time it will create an uncertain scenario for all other trade partners, because, due to its size, it will establish a new system of rules, probably in conflict with the WTO because it will discriminate between elements that are included and elements that are excluded from this PTA. New rules will occur in areas expanding WTO rules (WTO-plus), such as services and intellectual property, but rules will also be generated in new areas, such as environment, climate change, labor, investment and competition (WTO-extra rules).

A study of current TTIP proposals demonstrates quite clearly that the main focus of this agreement will be on the elimination of non-tariff barriers and the creation of better regulatory coherence. The most important proclaimed achievement will be the construction of the 21st century trading system. For outsiders, this raises concerns regarding the role to be played by the WTO.

The Growth of Preferential Trade Agreements

International trade is undergoing significant and complex change that represents a great challenge to Brazilian foreign trade policy. The deadlock in multilateral negotiations under the WTO Doha Round has led major players in international trade, notably the United States and the European Union, to focus on the negotiation of preferential trade agreements (PTAs), where they could advance trade rules, lower trade barriers and promote integration with their partners, signaling the rules they want for the present century.

Figure 1. Preferential Trade Agreements Notifications (1948–2012)

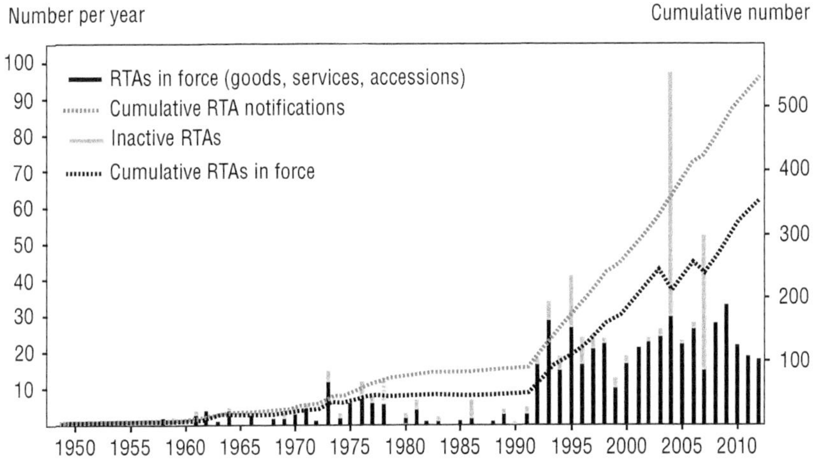

Number per year   Cumulative number

Source: WTO Secretariat.

Figure 1 shows that there has been a huge increase in the number of Preferential Trade Arrangements (PTAs) in the past years, pointing to the importance that these agreements have acquired in the regulation of international trade flows.

The first generation of PTAs sought to reduce or eliminate tariffs in goods between partners. This preferential access could either increase international trade flows, due to the market liberalization promoted by the agreement (trade creation) or to divert flows from more competitive players (trade diversion).

The following generation of PTAs has promoted, besides tariff reductions, the negotiation of rules on subjects not fully addressed by the multilateral system, establishing a relevant framework of trade regulation on the regional level, affecting not only the partners of the respective PTA, but also influencing multilateral negotiations.

The current generation of PTAs keeps the trends of the previous agreements, but go further. These deep-integration PTAs promote greater coordination and harmonization between trade partners, facilitating the establishment of production chains on the regional level, contributing to the major trade phenomenon of the 21st century:

global value chains. The TTIP between the EU and the United States, and the TPP between the United States, Australia, Brunei, Canada, Chile, Japan, Malaysia, Mexico, New Zealand, Peru, Singapore, and Vietnam, are the most ambitious negotiations of these next generation PTAs.

The negotiations of these two agreements present an ambitious agenda, with substantial elimination of tariffs in goods, enlargement of market access in services and government procurement, harmonization and mutual recognition of technical, sanitary and phytosanitary measures.

Besides ambitious schedules of preferential tariffs, modern PTAs have a broad regulatory framework to deal with bilateral international trade flows of goods and services. This set of rules deals with several trade-related activities and may have a direct impact on market access of the preferential trade partners. These rules, whether WTO-plus or WTO-extra, often surpass the scope of the agreements of the multilateral trading system, and encompass themes not regulated by the WTO.

This proliferation of PTAs, with rules that promote deep integration between partners, has an important effect on international trade flows, since countries that participate in these agreements have a wider market access, provided both by the reduction of tariff and non-tariff barriers, as well as harmonization of trade rules, trade facilitation, and other factors. Yet countries that do not participate in any PTA tend to suffer losses in their share of exports to other countries, because products from preferential partners have preferential access, and can be more competitive when enjoying the benefits conferred by the PTA.

Preferential Trade Agreements and Brazil

For many years Brazil has prioritized multilateral negotiations in detriment of preferential ones. The rationale behind this option was that the country would have greater bargaining power if negotiating in the multilateral forum together with other developing countries. But with the stalemate of the Doha Round, Brazil needs to change its strategy and reformulate its trade policy. Two priorities deserve deep discussion: the participation of Brazil in new PTAs and the participation of Brazil in a world of global value chains. Immobilization will result in the isolation of Brazil in international trade.

A relevant issue for the Brazilian agricultural sector will be the negotiation by the EU of preferential tariff quotas for the United States. These quotas shall impact and reduce the global tariff quotas offered by the EU in its agricultural market and can significantly harm Brazilian exports.

In addition, the enlargement of market access of the trade partners participating in these two agreements shall have as an effect not only the increase in trade flows between these parties, but can also reduce flows from other players such as Brazil to these destinations (trade diversion), since Brazilian products will not face this privileged market access.

The agreements will also include several WTO-plus and WTO-extra rules such as enhanced intellectual property protection, as proposed by the United States in the TPP, regulation of e-commerce, competition rules, liberalization and protection of investments, regulation of trade related aspects of state owned enterprises, provisions on small and medium sized enterprises, rules of international supply chains, among other themes.[2] One major concern in the development of WTO-plus rules in PTAs is that they will eventually affect all trade players and not only the ones that have directly participated in the negotiation of the PTA.

The rules of deep integration negotiated within those agreements, which regulate behind-the-border barriers, such as technical regulations and intellectual property, are likely to be extended to all other players, since these rules imply in a modification of the countries' national legislation to be applied to all goods or services trade within the territory of the respective country. Therefore, Brazilian products are likely to face technical and sanitary standards negotiated within the TTIP or

---

[2]Fergusson I, Cooper, W., Jurenas, R., and Williams, B., *The Trans Pacific Partnership Negotiations and Issues for Congress*, Congressional Research Service Report for Congress, June 2013, pp. 47–48; and *Interim Report to Leaders from the Co-Chairs EU-US High Level Working Group on Jobs and Growth*, June 2012.

enhanced intellectual property protection in patents registered in any of the TPP partners, which may also damage Brazilian exports.

Brazil will have to adapt to several of the requirements present in these two agreements without having participated in the drafting such rules, and thus, without being able to advance its own interests and perspectives in the regulation of such themes. Therefore, if the country does not participate in this movement toward negotiation of 21st century PTAs, it will become a rule-taker instead of a rule-maker, bearing all the costs related to its late arrival to this new generation of international trade rules.

The TPP and the TTIP are likely to promote much deeper economic integration among their respective members, resulting in the elimination of several trade barriers, regulatory harmonization, and creation of regional value chains. The benefits of this deep integration include an increase in business opportunities (trade in goods and services and investments) among the partners as well as the exchange of know-how and technology through the internationalized production chain, enhancing the countries' competitiveness and negatively affecting trade partners that do not participate in this process of regional integration.

This chapter presents simulations that show the costs of Brazil's isolation. Assuming that Brazil does not sign any PTA with significant trade partners, and that the TTIP enters into force, this chapter presents the impact of these agreements on Brazil's productive sectors and its main macroeconomic variables.

TTIP and Brazil

This chapter analyzes TTIP's implications for Brazil by considering four different hypotheses. The first considers the effects on Brazil of a TTIP that only reduces U.S.-EU tariff barriers. The second considers the effects of tariff reduction plus a partial reduction of non-tariff barriers. The third examines the implications of a complete reduction of these barriers. A final "audacious" alternative is assumed in which Brazil participates in the TTIP under both a partial reduction of agricultural tariffs by the U.S. and EU markets, and under a full liberalization of their agricultural markets.[3]

Simulation 1—Impact of TTIP on Brazil

This simulation presents the impact of the TTIP negotiations on the Brazilian economy. Three different hypotheses are proposed: (i) a full tariff reduction between the United States and the EU; (ii) full tariff elimination plus a 50% reduction of non-tariff barriers (NTB); and (iii) full elimination of both tariffs and NTBs.

Results

Under the first hypothesis—full tariff reduction only between the United States and the EU—Brazilian exports to the United States and the EU fall by 0.6%, a decrease of of $0.4 billion. Brazilian imports from the United States and the EU would fall by 0.4%, a decrease of $0.3 billion.

Under the second hypothesis—full U.S.-EU tariff elimination plus a 50% reduction of U.S.-EU non-tariff barriers (NTB), the most probable scenario—Brazil's exports to the United States and the EU fall by 5%, a decrease of $3.8 billion. Brazilian imports from the United States and the EU would fall by 4%, a decrease of $3.1 billion.

Under the third hypothesis—full elimination of both U.S.-EU tariffs and NTBs—Brazil's exports to the United States and the EU fall by 10%, a decrease of $7.8 billion. Brazilian imports from the United States and the EU would fall by 8%, a decrease of $6.4 billion.

These comparisons indicate the opportunities lost to Brazil by remaining outside such negotiations. In addition, since a TTIP agreement is likely to boost U.S. and EU competitiveness and spark additional U.S. and EU exports, Brazil's overall share of world trade is likely to decline.

The simulation also presents differing results for particular sectors.

---

[3]The methodology used to estimate non-tariff barriers was adopted from Ecorys, *Non-Tariff Measures in EU-US Trade and Investment—An Economic Analysis*, Report prepared for the European Commission, 2009, http://trade.ec.europa.eu/doclib/docs/2009/december/tradoc_145613.pdf

TTIP results in small losses for most of Brazil's agricultural sectors, with a slightly better scenario according to the level of liberalization of NTBs. One factor that should affect Brazilian agricultural exports to the EU is that any preferential tariff quotas offered by the EU to the United States should affect other countries' market access to the EU, since the global tariff quotas will be shared by many partners, with the United States benefiting from a larger share of such a global quotas. The simulation indicates that Brazilian agricilture would benefit from the elimination of U.S-EU NTBs.

For Brazilian industry, TTIP results are mixed, with in gains for a number of sectors and losses for others. This can be explained by the fact that the increase of trade flows and economic integration between the EU and the United States would create some demand for exports from other countries as well.

When the elimination of U.S.-EU non-tariff barriers is taken into account, the negative impact to Brazil is more significant with regard to sectoral GDP and trade flows. The trade gains of TTIP will be obtained less through tariff negotiations than through negotiations of non-tariff barriers, including technical barriers, sanitary and phytosanitary measures, trade facilitation, among others, which nowadays are the real barriers to trade.

Considering only the elimination of only tariff barriers in the TTIP, the simulation shows that the impacts on Brazil is negative, but not too significant, representing:

1. losses of around 1% in GDP in 16 agrobusiness sectors of 20 sectors considered.

2. losses of around 1% in GDP in 9 industrial sectors of 21 sectors considered.

3. losses in the trade balance in 14 agrobusiness sectors of 20 sectors considered, mainly coffee, meat and meat products.

4. losses in the trade balance in 8 industrial sectors of 21 sectors considered, mainly leather products, non-metallic products, and motor vehicles and components.

Under the hypothesis of tariff elimination and a 50% reduction on NTB, the results are:

1. losses of 1%–3% in GDP in 15 agrobusiness sectors of 20 sectors considered.

2. losses of 1%–2% in GDP in 14 industrial sectors of 21 sectors considered.

3. losses in the trade balance in 14 agrobusiness sectors of 20 sectors considered, mainly soya, animal feed, coffee, meat and meat products.

4. losses in the trade balance in 8 industrial sectors of 21 sectors considered, mainly leather products, non-metallic products, motor vehicles and components, and transport material.

Simulation 2—Impact of Brazil's Participation in TTIP on the Brazilian Economy

This "audacious" simulation presents the impact to the Brazilian economy of a hypothetical participation of the country in the TTIP negotiations.

The hypothesis assumed for such participation are: (i) a full liberalization of both tariff and NTBs; (ii) a 50% reduction of tariffs in agriculture for the United States and the EU and a full liberalization of all other tariffs and NTBs; and (iii) a 50% liberalization of the EU and U.S. agricultural sectors, 50% liberalization of Brazil's industry and services and a full liberalization of non-tariff barriers for all partners.

When Brazil adheres to the TTIP, its exports register a significant increase:

1. a full liberalization of tariffs and NTBs for TTIP results in a strong increase of 126% of Brazilian exports, corresponding to a $95.4 billion raise.

2. a 50% reduction of agricultural tariffs plus a full liberalization of all other tariffs and NTBs results in an increase of 102% of the country's exports, corresponding to $77.3 billion.

3. a 50% reduction of EU and U.S. agricultural tariffs, a 50% reduction of Brazilian industrial tariffs and a full liberalization of non-tariff barriers for all partners, boost Brazilian exports by 121%, corresponding to $91.5 billion.

    4. finally, in a more realistic scenario of 50% reduction of EU and U.S. agricultural tariffs, a 50% reduction of Brazilian industrial tariffs and a 50% reduction of non-tariff barriers for all partners, Brazilian exports increase by 67.6%, corresponding to $51.1 billion.[4]

In the TTIP, there is a very noticeable increase in the exports of agricultural products, which explains the gains in the land value and the valorization of the Brazilian real.

Regarding imports, when Brazil participates in the TTIP:

    1. full liberalization of tariffs and NTBs results in an increase of 54% increase in Brazilian imports from the United States and the EU, a $43.1 billion rise.

    2. a 50% liberalization in agricultural tariffs and a full liberalization in other tariffs and NTBs results in a 46.5% increase in Brazilian imports from the United States and the European Union, a rise of $37.2 billion.

    3. a 50% liberalization of the U.S. and EU agricultural sectors, a 50% liberalization in the Brazilian industrial sector and a full liberalization of non-tariff barriers for all partners results in a 34.9% increase in Brazilian imports from the United States and the EU, a rise of $27.9 billion.

    4. finally, in a more realistic scenario of 50% reduction of EU and U.S. agricultural tariffs, a 50% reduction of Brazilian industrial tariffs and a 50% reduction of non-tariff barriers for all partners, Brazilian imports from the United States and the EU increase by 52.9%, a rise of $ 42.3 billion.[5]

The second simulation also presents different results for particular sectors of the economy.

Assuming Brazilian participation in TTIP, there are highly significant gains for the majority of Brazil's agricultural sectors in all three scenarios. This presents the greatest opportunity costs of Brazil remaining outside the transatlantic integration process.

------

[4]Values from Secex (US$ F.O.B.) for 2012.

[5]Ibid.

The impact on Brazilian industry is mixed, with both losses and gains, partly due to the impact of exchange rates.

The audacious hypothesis of including Brazil as a part of TTIP presents a substantial gain for Brazilian agriculture, but as expected, losses for several of Brazil's industrial sectors due to the overvaluation of exchange rates and the consequent increase of industrial imports. To make this hypothesis viable, two important tasks are needed: the Brazilian industry must face arduous work to improve its competitiveness, and the Brazilian government should also play its role through active economic policies.

In summary:

1. gains from 3% to more than 4% in GDP in 13 agrobusiness sectors of 20 sectors considered.

2. losses of 1% to 3% in GDP in 19 industrial sectors of 21 sectors considered.

3. gains in the trade balance in 13 agrobusiness sectors of 21 sectors considered, mainly soya, animal feed, vegetal oils, coffee, meat and meat products.

4. gains in the trade balance in 8 industrial sectors of 21 sectors considered, mainly leather products, petroleum products; and

5. losses in the trade balance of paper and pulp, chemical, non-metallic products, motor vehicles and components, machinery and electronic products.

Conclusion of a U.S.-EU TTIP without Brazilian integration into pan-Atlantic commerce will represent a serious threat to Brazil. Not only will Brazil lose international markets, it will be left behind in the negotiations of international trade rules. It will lose its present role as relevant global rule-maker and assume a secondary role as passive rule-taker.

In a time of global value chains, Brazil's integration with these two major economies is fundamental to the survival of Brazilian industry.

The analysis presented in this chapter shows clearly that the negotiation of an agreement between Brazil and the EU, now in its final phase, is an important step forward and should be concluded rapidly, before the finalization of the TTIP negotiations.

But a second step should also be considered seriously—that of an agreement with the United States. There is no "trade logic" in an agreement with the EU without an agreement with the United States in the case of a succesfull TTIP.

With the TTIP, a new opportunity is open to Brazil. It is time for Brazil to review its priorities and to reevaluate losses and gains. The costs of Brazil´s isolation in the world because of Mercosul's difficulties should be re-examined with care. It is time for action!

Technical Annex:
Simulations on the Impact of TTIP for Brazil

The GTAP computable general equilibrium model was used in the simulations to evaluate the first round effects of the costs and opportunities for Brazil of the conclusion of the TTIP.[6] The GTAP model is a global comparative static applied general equilibrium model. The model identifies 57 sectors in 153 regions of the world. Its system of equations is based on microeconomic foundations providing a detailed specification of household and perfect competitive firm behavior within individual regions and trade linkages between regions. In addition to trade flows the GTAP model also recognizes global transportation costs.

The GTAP model qualifies as a Johansen-type model. This model estimates the impacts of external shocks (gains and losses of a PTA) through a comparative static modeling (before and after the shock). The solutions are obtained by solving the system of linearized equations of the model. A typical result shows the percentage change in the set of endogenous variables (GDP, exports and imports, exchange rate and land value) after a policy shock is carried out, compared to their values in the initial equilibrium, in a given environment. The schematic presentation of Johansen solutions for such models is standard in the literature.[7]

The GTAP 8 database combines detailed bilateral trade, transport and protection data characterizing economic linkages among 129

---

[6]For a description of the standard GTAP model, see Hertel, T.W., *Global Trade Analysis: Modeling and Applications*. Cambridge: Cambridge University Press, 1997.

[7]See Dixon, P. B., Parmenter, B. R., Powell, A. A., & Wilcoxen, P. J., "Notes and Problems in Applied General Equilibrium Economics," in C. J. Bliss & M. D. Intriligator (eds.), *Advanced*

regions, together with individual country input-output data bases which account for inter-sectorial linkages within regions. The dataset is harmonized and completed with additional sources to provide the most accurate description of the world economy in 2007 (the last available data base for GTAP).

The main applied protection data used in the GTAP 8 data base originates from ITC's MacMap database, which contains exhaustive information at the tariff line level. The ITC database includes the United Nations Conference on Trade and Development's (UNC-TAD's) Trade Analysis and information system (TRAINS) data base, to which ITC staff added their own data. The model transforms all specific tariffs in ad valorem tariffs.

In order to capture the first round effects, the simulations were carried out using a standard GTAP hypothesis, which considers perfect factor mobility for labor and capital and imperfect factor mobility for land and natural resources. National aggregate supply of factors of production is exogenous and production technology for firms is given.

The way the economy variables are affected by horizontal reductions in bilateral import tariffs of the TTIP partners will depend on the resulting behavior of domestic relative prices. Domestic relative prices of the TTIP partners will be altered in such a way that import competition from the PTA partner will be favored, as the economy becomes more preferentially open to trade. Overall efficiency in resource allocation tends to be improved and, by the same token, possible gains from trade may take national welfare a step up.

Notwithstanding the aggregate benefits from improved resource allocation, regions might be adversely affected through re-orientation of trade flows—trade diversion—as relative accessibility changes in the system. Thus bilateral aggregate gains from trade are not necessarily accompanied by generalized regional gains in welfare. This issue of trade diversion versus trade creation has been an important one in the international trade literature, especially in the case of welfare evaluations of preferential trade agreements.

Textbooks in Economics vol. 32. Amsterdam: North-Holland, 1992; and Dixon, P. B.,& Parmenter, B. R., "Computable General Equilibrium Modelling for Policy Analysis and Forecasting," in H. M. Amman, D. A. Kendrick, & J. Rust (eds.), *Handbook of Computational Economics* vol. 1, pp. 3–85. Amsterdam: Elsevier, 1996.

Chapter 11

TTIP and Sub-Saharan Africa: A Proposal to Harmonize EU and U.S. Preferences

Eveline Herfkens

The Transatlantic Trade and Investment Partnership (TTIP) has generated a great deal of commentary about its economic potential for the EU and the United States. Much less consideration has been given to its impact on third countries and the global trading system. Will a preferential trade agreement covering so much of world trade, further undermine the multilateral trading system, sucking negotiating energy out of the WTO, just as the WTO, following its Bali Ministerial, appears to be recovering from its slide to irrelevance?

Preferential trade agreements (PTAs) discriminate against non-participants, as they may divert trade from cheaper non-member to more expensive member sources. Poor non-members, currently enjoying preferences, see their preferential margins erode, as overall levels of protection are reduced. To what extent will a TTIP lead to trade diversion at the expense of third countries, especially poor ones? Will there be offsetting positive effects? Obviously, if tariffs and non-tariff barriers between the United States and the EU decline or are eliminated, the relative barriers to market entry faced by third countries become higher. The evidence on trade diversion of previous PTAs is quite mixed. The WTO in a comprehensive review reported significant trade diversion in some cases (MERCOSUR vis-à-vis the Caribbean) and little in others.[1]

The highly concentrated nature of exports from Sub-Saharan Africa (SSA) implies that the erosion of preferences in a small set of specific product categories (textiles, clothing and footwear[2] and spe-

---

[1] WTO, World Trade Report, *The WTO and Preferential Trade Agreements: from Coexistence to Coherence* (Geneva, 2011).

[2] EU and U.S. tariffs are typically more (and often much more) than 10% on textiles and clothing.

cific agricultural products such as fish, bananas and sugar) can have important negative consequences for these countries. More rigorous standards might be more difficult to comply with or even lock out SSA exporters. And more advanced intellectual property rules might affect the introduction and production of generic drugs and their supplies to SSA.

One of the few efforts to quantify the potential impact of a TTIP has been undertaken by the Bertelsmann Stiftung. Its report, *Transatlantic Trade and Investment Partnership (TTIP): Who benefits from a free trade deal?*[3], predicts that the main losers will be developing countries including Sub-Sahara Africa, a region that contains most of the world's poorest countries. If that were allowed to happen it would be contrary to existing European and U.S. policies, which aim, however imperfectly, to improve market access and export prospects for Sub-Saharan Africa.

At present both the United States and the EU operate a complex set of preferential trade arrangements vis-à-vis Sub-Saharan Africa. The TTIP creates the opportunity to codify, align and extend these arrangements instead of undermining them; and it can do so as a part of the architecture from the outset, not as an afterthought following years of exclusive negotiations. This chapter focuses on how TTIP can be used to help rather than hinder Sub-Sahara Africa, the region that not only has most to fear from a TTIP, but also most desperately needs generous access to rich country markets. Caring about SSA would be consistent with core Western values. And showing compassion is the more opportune, as the West is losing the battle for African "hearts & minds."

Sub-Saharan Africa's Trade and the TTIP

Sub-Saharan Africa needs to expand exports in order to create jobs, raise incomes, and, ultimately, reduce poverty and aid dependency. Domestic markets in most SSA countries are simply too small to enable local industry to achieve economies of scale. Increased trade

---

[3]Bertelsmann Stiftung, *Transatlantic Trade and Investment Partnership (TTIP): Who Benefits from a Free Trade Deal?* (Gütersloh, 2013).

opportunities would encourage both domestic and foreign investment that is critical to long term development.

The region's exports have been growing rapidly, about 14% per annum in the last decade. But the bulk of the growth has come from increased exports of oil and raw materials. The important emergence of global value chains virtually bypassed the region: by 2010 SSA had lower ratios of parts and components in its imports than in 1980.[4] And its overall share of world trade is a miniscule 2.2%. This marginalization of the region is critical in holding back its development.

For SSA to improve its capacity to exploit trade opportunities and diversify its economies, many obstacles have to be tackled: first and foremost it is critical to establish a single common regional market to reduce "internal" trade costs.[5] In addition, much remains to be done regarding the supply side: investment is needed in reliable energy; in infrastructure to reduce transport costs; in human capital and institutional capacity; and in general in improving the investment and business environment.

Africa's improved trade and economic performance over the last decade shows that many of these issues are in fact being addressed. But more can also be done to improve the external environment.

Trade policies around the world discriminate against the manufacturing and agricultural exports of poor countries. Average tariffs in rich countries are in the low single digits, but tariffs are still high in sectors where poor countries do well. This is supposedly being addressed by preferential schemes offered by the EU to the least developed countries (LDCs),[6] and, in the case of the United States, to a larger group of countries in Sub-Saharan Africa. But the utilization of the European scheme has been quite limited and in the case of the U.S. scheme, relevant products are excluded and those countries that need preferences most have not benefitted significantly from them.

---

[4] C. Michalopoulos, *Emerging Powers in the WTO* (Houndsmills: Palgrave/ Macmillan, 2013).

[5] P. Collier and A. Venables, "Rethinking Trade Preferences: How Africa Can Diversify its Exports," *The World Economy*, 30(8), 2007, pp. 1326-45.

[6] These are the 49 countries that meet the UN criteria involving per capita income, industrial and human development indices, 27 of these are in Sub-Sahara Africa.

From the standpoint of a foreign investor deciding on a project, an African exporter looking for markets or an African government official deciding on policy, the present hodgepodge system of preferences is a nightmare: different schemes cover different countries, with different product coverage and different rules of origin. No wonder transaction costs in Africa are high.

On top of this, the TTIP, by providing preferences to U.S. and European exporters, would undercut SSA access to both markets. How big the effect will depend on the TTIP design. The Bertelsmann report suggests that the poorer countries would suffer, particularly Africa, as their exports to Europe would be pushed out by goods from the United States. African countries will also be among the largest net losers from reduction in non-tariff barriers if the TTIP succeeds in creating "deep liberalization."

The report from a "Transatlantic Task Force on Trade and Investment"[7] promoting the TTIP acknowledges that "the capacity of such an agreement to generate positive systemic consequences, and improve conditions for trade beyond the Atlantic region, depends on the design of a transatlantic trade agreement and how it links up with common EU and U.S. initiatives with other countries." The Task Force advocates that TTIP should address the integration, harmonization and modernization of their current preferential trade agreements (PTAs) with third countries, to "limit the negative effects of trade diversion and help to reduce so-called "spaghetti-bowl" effects.

If the United States and the EU do not want the TTIP to harm the poorest continent, it would be best for their relations with SSA, to deal with this now, as a precursor to an overall agreement, rather than as just one of many issues on the EU-US negotiation agenda somewhere in the future.

The TTIP provides an opportunity to rationalize country, product coverage and rules of U.S. and EU preferential schemes[8] towards SSA

---

[7]"A New Era for Transatlantic Trade Leadership," Report from the Transatlantic Task Force on Trade and Investment, co-chaired by Ewa Björling and Jim Kolbe, The European Centre for International Political Economy (ECIPE) and the German Marshall Fund of the United States (GMF), 2012.

[8]The African Union Conference of Ministers of Trade (2011, Accra) produced a "Proposal for a Common and Enhanced Trade Preference System for Least Developed Countries

that need to be done any way. This chapter presents a proposal that would not just minimize further erosion of SSA market access, but improve, harmonize and modernize present schemes by establishing one common and generous system of trade preferences for low and lower middle income Sub-Saharan African country exports into the European and U.S. markets.

U.S. and European Trade Preferences Schemes for Sub-Saharan Africa

At present there are several different preferential trade arrangements in favor of low income and least developed countries in Africa, with different country and product coverage and different requirements regarding the rules of origin that permit goods to qualify for preferential treatment.[9] The complexity of these arrangements presents serious challenges for countries in Africa with limited institutional capacity. As a consequence, their utilization of the preferences is limited and the benefits they derive are much less than they could be.

U.S. Scheme: The African Growth and Opportunity Act (AGOA)

AGOA was signed into law on May 18, 2000 as Title 1 of The Trade and Development Act of 2000 and extended until September 30, 2015.

AGOA's *country eligibility* requirements are onerous. The Act authorizes the President to designate countries as eligible to receive the benefits of AGOA if they are *inter alia* determined to have established, or are making continual progress toward establishing market-based economies, the rule of law and political pluralism; elimination of barriers to U.S. trade and investment; protection of intellectual

---

(LDC's) and Low Income Countries (LIC's)". www.au.int/en/sites/default/files/TI6204%20_E%20Original%20TD11.doc). As the beneficiaries of this proposal would not be limited to SSA, in order to ensure compatibility with WTO rules it suggests the prior establishment of a custom union among LDCs, a prohibitive requirement, given the daunting challenges of such a process.

[9]In addition to the schemes focused on Africa and the LDCs, developed countries have also established so called Generalized Schemes of Preferences (GSP) for developing countries more generally, which however, typically involve less advantageous preferences and product coverage.

property; combating corruption; policies to reduce poverty, protection of human rights and worker rights. Recognizing the progress Sub-Saharan African countries have been making in these areas, AGOA provides at present preferred access to the U.S. market for 40 of the 48 Sub-Saharan African countries. Among those excluded are Sudan, the Central African Republic, Eritrea and Zimbabwe.

However, as eligibility is not limited to relatively poor countries, AGOA includes the Upper Middle Income Countries (UMIC) in the region[10] with per capita incomes above $4000, which are much better positioned to make use of such preferences. The countries that really need preferences hardly benefit: 90% percent of SSA exports under AGOA consists of petroleum products. Of the $3.5 billion in non-oil AGOA exports in 2008, about $2 billion were automobiles, manufactured in South Africa[11] with massive domestic subsidies and limited job creation.[12] Just over $1 billion was clothing, mostly from Kenya, Lesotho, Madagascar, Mauritius, and Swaziland.[13]

AGOA's *product coverage* is less than generous. It removes tariffs on roughly 98% of products, but excludes key agricultural products, such as cotton, exactly those in which poor African countries have a comparative advantage and the sector that employs the vast majority of the poor. Restrictions on imports of sugar and dairy products discourage African cocoa exporters from processing cocoa beans into chocolate and other value-added products. As with all preferential schemes, there are complex rules of origin which limit the number of products eligible for preferential treatment (see below).

Another problem with AGOA is that the preferences are granted through an unpredictable political process and for a limited time. This uncertainty deters both exporters and investors. The program is

---

[10]Angola; Botswana; Gabon; Mauritius; Namibia; the Seychelles; and South Africa.

[11]Kimberly Elliot, "Open Markets for the Poorest Countries: Trade Preferences That Work," CGD Working Group on Global Trade Preference Reform (Washington, DC: Center for Global Development, 2010), of which the author was a member.

[12]IPS, http://www.ipsnews.net/2013/04/should-south-african-taxpayers-subsidise-car-making-robots/.

[13]Kimberly Elliot, "Reviving AGOA," CDG Brief (Washington, DC: Center for Global Development, 2010).

scheduled to expire in 2015; and while the U.S. Administration is committed to renewal, the decision is up to Congress.

European Preferential Schemes

Everything But Arms (EBA)

EBA entered into force on March 5, 2001. It allows all imports to the EU from the LDCs duty free and quota free (DFQF), i.e. completely free access except for *armaments*.

Country coverage is limited to the group of Least Developed Countries (LDCs), which encompasses 27 countries in Sub-Saharan Africa. This is problematic, as regional integration is presently high on the political agenda of SSA—as it should be. But these efforts[14] span both LDCs and non-LDCs (e.g. Ghana, Kenya, and Nigeria), complicating the creation of truly common markets in the region. More fundamentally, by limiting this preferential access to LDCs, EBA excludes the countries that are low-income, such as Kenya, or lower middle income,[15] which are precisely those African countries best-placed to take advantage of preferences for export diversification.[16]

The present disaggregation of industrial production processes across several countries has potential for the region.[17] But the economies of poor small countries are simply too narrow. In order to be able to specialize in a limited range of activities (or transformation steps) and participate in global value chains, they must be able to rely on their neighbors to provide necessary inputs. Excluding the most feasible locations (Kenya, Ghana) also denies opportunities for their poorer neighbors (Tanzania, Liberia).

---

[14]ECOWAS, the Economic Community of West African States; CEMAC, la Communauté Economic et Monétaire de l'Afrique Central; SADC, the Southern African Development Community; EAC, the East African Development Community and ESA (Eastern and Southern Africa),

[15]Cameroon; Cape Verde; Congo; Cote d'Ivoire; Ghana; Lesotho; Nigeria; Sao Tome and Principe; Senegal; South Sudan, Sudan; Swaziland and Zambia.

[16]D.G. Greenaway, P. Collier, and A. Venables, "Rethinking Trade Preferences: How Africa Can Diversify its Exports," *The World Economy*, Chapter 7, "Global Trade Policy," 2009.

[17]Ibid.

Product coverage is very generous (99.8%); currently it only excludes arms and ammunitions. The complexity of its rules of origin has recently led the EU to efforts to improve liberalize them without visible improvements (see below).

European Partnerships Agreements (EPAs)

For decades the EU has granted preferential access to its market for former colonies in Africa, the Pacific and the Caribbean (ACP countries). As these preferential arrangements became apparently incompatible with WTO rules, since 2002 the EU has been trying to replace them with "Economic Partnership Agreements" with regional groupings in SSA, the Pacific and the Caribbean, which are reciprocal, and presumably open to all developing countries in the region.

This course of action was unfortunate for several reasons. Given the limited capacity for trade negotiations of most countries in the region, their efforts should have focused on deeper integration within the African market and on the much more relevant Doha Round.

Moreover, the requirement of reciprocity and coverage of substantial all trade in such agreements (as required by Article 24 of the WTO) was probably unnecessary, given the state of development of most of the region and the way Article 24 has been applied. The EU also included issues that go beyond trade in goods (services, intellectual property, government procurement, abolishing export duties, etc.) which will create unnecessarily burdensome obligations for these countries and may distract from or could be inconsistent with their more immediate development priorities.

The membership of the various African regional groupings overlaps; and most of them include LDCs that already have access through the EBA scheme, creating problems for groupings that have common external tariffs.

It is no surprise that, though a few interim-agreements were signed, since the launch of EPA negotiations in 2002, with January1, 2008 as deadline, no EPA has been ratified with any of the African groupings. A deal was signed only with the ECOWAS Commission, but this Commission lacks the authority to ratify or implement the EPA and many African countries do not see the rationale for continuing negotiations on them. In the meantime the EU has upped the stakes by threatening to remove from the current duty free treatment under Regulation 1528/2007 by October 1, 2014 those non least developed countries that have not ratified and implemented their interim EPA.

The time has come for the EU to reconsider its trade policy vis-à-vis Sub-Saharan Africa.

Rules of Origin

All preference schemes are underutilized, some more than others. Partly this is because of supply constraints. But a common problem is the complexity of requirements exporters need to meet to benefit with regard to the preferential rules of origin (RoO). The WTO recognized the need to simplify RoO in its Ministerial Conference in Bali. Alas, the 2013 Ministerial Decision lacks any commitment ("Members should endeavor") and is only applicable to the limited group of LDCs.[18]

The purpose of the rules is to prevent "trade deflection" or simple transshipment, where products from non-beneficiary countries are re-directed through a preference beneficiary, perhaps with minimal working and relabeling to avoid payment of higher customs duties. Rules of origin define how much processing must take place locally before goods and materials are considered to be the product of the exporting country and be rewarded with preferential market access.

This sounds simple enough but it in practice is a daunting obstacle. First, RoO can raise production costs, if, to meet the requirements, (parts of) the product must be produced in a different manner or place, than would be the case otherwise. Second, exporters have to adhere to documentation requirements, based on (at times) complicated cost accounting and apportionment, detailed and lengthy record keeping, exporter registration and so forth. Administrative costs are not limited to traders, but also represent a burden to customs authorities with limited institutional capacity. The ad valorem cost of RoO is estimated to be about 4%.[19]

---

[18]WTO, 2013. *Ministerial Conference: Ninth Session, Bali, 3-6 December, WT/MIN(13)/42, WT/L/917* (Geneva: WTO, 2013).

[19]J. Francois, B. Hoekman and Manchin, "Preference Erosion and Multilateral Trade Liberalization," *World Bank Economic Review* 20 (2), 2006.

Rules of Origin in the EU EBA Scheme

In the case of the EBA scheme the rules of origin defined access so restrictively and inflexibly, that the scheme was under-utilized and had minimal impact on LDC exports to the EU. A decade after the introduction of EBA the European Commission acknowledged "a correlation was indeed proven between the stringency of the rules of origin and the utilization rates of the tariff preferences. In addition, product specific rules were considered too complicated. Lastly, compliance was considered too costly and burdensome, both for exporters and administrations."[1] The EU introduced revised rules of origin as of January 1, 2011, simplifying and liberalizing the rules for EBA beneficiaries. For example, for most industrial products, the threshold of valued-added required from LDCs was reduced to 30% (against 50% per cent for non-LDCs). For textiles and clothing, single transformation has been granted without quotas. And EBA's cumulation provisions were changed to facilitate limited cumulation between countries of a regional group with different levels of market access to the EU. To what extent these changes are sufficient to increase utilization remains to be seen.

---

[1]S.Laird, "A Review of Trade Preference Schemes for the World's Poorest Countries," Issue Paper 25 (Geneva: ICTSD, 2012), p. 35.

A third problem with RoO is that preference granting countries employ substantially *different methodologies* to define origin (a specific proportion of the total value added; and/or that the product has undergone sufficient transformation so as to be classified in a different tariff category). This obliges beneficiary producers to adapt their manufacturing processes in order to comply with the various conditions that they impose, sometimes incompatible with each other and/or substantially different.

As a result, developing countries are faced with a myriad of rules, depending on the export destination. For example, an exporter based in Tanzania will face different rules when exporting goods to Europe or the United States, each of which also differs when compared to the RoO under the regional COMESA trade agreement.

The differences in these rules impedes diversification in Sub-Saharan Africa, as it is easier to diversify by selling products that have been successfully sold in one market into other markets than selling different products into more markets, as new investments may be needed to penetrate each new market.[20]

The fourth and most fundamental problem with current RoO is that, since their creation decades ago, the world globalized: production of a good became fragmented between many countries, with each specializing in one narrow task. Comparative advantages are less and less at the level of whole products, but simply a specific transformation step. As Pascal Lamy has phrased it, "Global value chains have profoundly changed the way we trade. Whereas before we traded in goods, today we trade in tasks."[21] UNCTAD's 2013 *World Investment Report* shows how global value chains form the nexus between trade and investment: the vast majority of global trade—some 80%—is linked to the international production networks of transnational corporations.[22]

By requiring substantial value added, RoO can be prohibitive to participate in global value chains, as SSA typically has limited industrial capacity. RoO based on the assumption that a poor country can create a significant share of value added are unrealistic and a strong limitation in promoting manufacturing specialization. The reality is that in Sub-Saharan Africa few inputs are available domestically: the economies are narrow and need to rely on their neighbors to provide necessary inputs.[23]

One way to deal with this problem is for preferential schemes to permit *cumulation*. This allows inputs from other countries within a cumulation zone to be counted as being of local origin when further

---

[20]Ibid., p. 10. This helps explain why Lesotho has significant exports of apparel to the United States, but not to the EU.

[21]Pascal Lamy, http://www.ipsnews.net/2013/08/the-world-trade-organisation-after-eight-transformational-years/.

[22]UNCTAD, *World Investment Report 2013*, http://unctad.org/en/PublicationsLibrary/wir2013_en.pdf.

[23]Francois et. al, op cit., p.7.

processed there. *Bilateral* cumulation between the preference-giving and preference-receiving countries also allows inputs sourced from the one party to be considered as originating in the exporting country (and thus counted as local content) when further processed there. *Regional* cumulation permits countries in a regional group to contribute products for further processing by regional trade partners, thus reducing the restrictiveness of the relevant RoO. Regional cumulation is particularly relevant, in the case of schemes limited to LDCs, which often belong to the same Customs Unions (e.g. the East African Community (EAC) and the Southern African Customs Union (SACU), with non-LDC neighbors, which thus need to be included in expanded cumulation.

To allow cumulation is helpful in addressing the problem of limited value added in processing, but adds another layer of complexity in the documentation needed to ensure that a particular product is eligible for preferences as the origin of all the inputs needs to be traced and documented.

Global value chains offer potential for Africa, since it is much easier to develop capabilities in a narrow range of tasks than in integrated, vertical production of an entire product.[24] But for trade preferences to able to act as a catalyst for manufacturing exports, they need to be designed to be consistent with international trade in fragmented tasks (as opposed to complete products) and need to be open to countries with sufficient levels of complementary inputs such as skills and infrastructure.

As labor intensive export manufacturing is the key to African job creation and growth, it is time to update trade preferences to be relevant to the current disaggregation of production processes across countries. Expanding the cumulation provisions for Sub-Saharan Africa could help unlock trade flows and improve the region's market access.

Recommendations

The key to reform is to adopt the best elements of the EU and U.S. schemes that have been effective in helping utilization of preferences and harmonize them.

---

[24]Greenaway, et. al, op. cit.

Rules of Origin in U.S. AGOA

The general rule of origin for AGOA with respect to non-apparel products is that the sum of the cost or value of materials produced in the beneficiary country plus the direct costs of processing must equal at least 35% of the appraised value of the article at the time of its entry into the United States. While the rules permit limited bilateral cumulation (up to 15% out of 35% of "local" materials may comprise U.S. materials) and full cumulation between AGOA beneficiaries, a value-added requirement of 35% is likely to be difficult for many small developing countries.

For apparel products, however, AGOA introduced a so-called special rule, allowing African clothing manufacturers flexibility in sourcing fabrics, provided beneficiary countries establish effective visa systems and institute required enforcement and verification procedures before any of their apparel exports to the United States can receive AGOA benefits.

26 poorer African countries exporting apparel to the United States were allowed to use fabric from any origin (single transformation) and still meet the criteria for preferential access. This simplification contributed to an increase in export volume of about 168% for the top seven beneficiaries or approximately four times as much as the 44% growth effect from the initial preference access under the Africa Growth Opportunity Act without the single transformation proving that a bold approach to rules of origin can provoke substantial supply responses from developing countries and help them build a more diversified export base.[1]

---

[1]World Bank, Doing Business 2013, http://www.doingbusiness.org/special-features/infograph.

Change Country Coverage

It is difficult to justify a U.S.-EU trade arrangement that provides different developing country treatment. What particular European or U.S. foreign policy interest would be served, for example, by the EU and the United States providing different access to Kenya's products?

In order for the initiative to benefit those countries that need it most, without excluding only slightly less poor countries that can make use of the preferences, the initiative should focus on all low income and lower middle-income countries in Sub-Saharan Africa, i.e. countries with per capita income less than $4,035, excluding higher middle income countries (World Bank Atlas classification). With no income per capita restrictions, the bulk of the benefits may go as they do in AGOA to countries, like South Africa, that do not need them. Thus, the United States should exclude the higher middle-income countries (notably South Africa) that presently qualify for AGOA, while the EU should expand its scheme, presently focused on LDCs only, to include all Lower and Lower Middle Income Countries in Sub Saharan Africa.

Product Coverage Should be 100% DFQF

Most SSA countries' exports are highly specialized, producing a very narrow scope of goods; in many cases, a few raw materials account for most of their exports.[25] Excluding even a small number of products can rob the initiative of any meaning,[26] since in most developed country markets 3% per cent of tariff lines cover 90-98% of exports from LDCs.[27]

In this respect the EU's EBA with its 100% coverage is far superior to the U.S. scheme. The exclusion of key agricultural products is a serious gap in the U.S. program: for sugar, tobacco, and peanut exporters, tight restrictions on access to the U.S. market constitute a serious barrier, the more as agriculture provides livelihoods for roughly two-thirds of all Africans. The U.S. AGOA needs to be expanded to include particularly those in which these countries have a comparative advantage: agriculture and labor-intensive manufacturing products, including apparel and footwear.

---

[25]Oil and gas (Angola, Chad, Equatorial Guinea, Sudan); iron ore (Mauritania); diamonds (Central Africa Republic, Liberia, Sierra Leone); copper (Zambia); aluminum (Mozambique); agricultural crops like cocoa (Sao Tome, Togo), cotton (Benin, Burkina Faso, Mali, Togo)

[26]A. Bouet, et. al, "The Costs and Benefits of Duty-Free, Quota-Free Market Access for Poor Countries: Who and What Matters," *CGD Working Paper* (Washington, DC: Center for Global Development, 2010).

[27]D. Laborde, "Looking for a Meaningful Duty Free Quota Free Market Access Initiative in the Doha Development Agenda," Issue Paper 4 (Geneva: ICTSD, 2008).

Ensure That the Preferential Rules of Origin Provide Genuine Market Access

For Sub-Saharan Africa to be able to exploit preferential access, qualification requirements have to be relevant, simple and harmonized across preference givers. Updating the preferential RoO to the realities of production networks that define trading conditions in the 21st century is long overdue, as is international agreement on the methodology to define origin in order to harmonize these rules.

Negotiations on RoO have been dragging on for many years at the WTO without any results. While regulatory alignment is an essential part of the trade agreement as envisaged between the EU and the United States, these negotiations will be complex and thus time consuming.

In the meantime, the unilateral rules that guide exports from Sub-Sahara Africa could be relaxed to ensure genuine utilization of preferential market access.

Generous cumulation should be allowed, preferably regional, i.e. all Sub-Saharan Africa. The simplest way to create the necessary flexibility, which does not need any negotiations among the TTIP partners,[28] would be *mutual recognition* of origin regimes across preference givers, accepting an import eligible in one market as eligible in any other. This should be feasible as the TTIP is expected to rely extensively on the principle of mutual recognition, given the extent to which the U.S. and EU regulatory approaches differ.

Ensure Better Transparency and Predictability, and Therefore, Promote Trade and Investment, by Making Preferences Permanent or Long Lasting

The uncertainty that is associated with preference regimes that are changed frequently and may expire if not renewed periodically by parliaments (e.g. AGOA) can have very negative effects on investment decisions.[29]

Ideally, in order to provide over a long time horizon, preferences should be granted on a permanent basis preferably by binding them in

---

[28]Elliot, "Open Markets," op. cit.

[29]N. Phelps, J. Stillwell and R. Wanjiru, "Broken chain? Foreign Direct Investment in the Kenyan Clothing Industry," *World Development* 37(2), 2008, pp. 314-325.

the WTO. If periodic reviews are unavoidable, they should be sufficiently long lasting (a minimum of 10 years) to provide the security to investors for real market access to materialize.

Conclusion

The timing is right for a new initiative to help Sub-Saharan Africa benefit from trading opportunities in today's increasingly globalized world. And it is particularly high time for the EU to reconsider its trade policies (EPAs) with SSA, as it seems that—even with the Commission threatening loss of all preferential market access—there is simply no appetite in Africa for this approach. Moreover, the EPA negotiations are disruptive to Africa's own regional integration efforts—which indeed should take precedent in the interest of development.

The new U.S.-EU Trade and Investment Partnership provides the ideal opportunity to improve market access for SSA by taking the best features and most effective provisions of their respective preference programs, making them compatible in terms of country and product coverage and by updating the rules to the current trading environment and agreeing to mutual recognition of rules of origin.

The TTIP would benefit from harmonization of agreements with third countries anyway. But instead of being just one of many issues on the EU-U.S. negotiations agenda somewhere in the future, focusing on the urgent needs of Sub-Saharan Africa now, as a precursor to the overall agreement, would help the region's economic transformation, give a tremendous push to its integration in the world economy, and lift millions of people out of poverty.

Such an action would help win "hearts and minds" in Africa. It would be in keeping with the spirit of the Marshall Plan, by which the United States allowed and even prompted Europe to prioritize regional economic integration, helping to create a Europe, closely bound in common purpose, premised on democratic governance, the free exchange of goods and services, and enduring transatlantic ties to the United States.[30]

---

[30]Hitchcock, "The Marshall Plan and the Creation of the West," in Melvyn P. Leffler and Odd Arne Westad, eds., *The Cambridge History of the Cold War* (New York and London: Cambridge University Press, 2010).

About the Authors

Lucas Ferraz is a professor at the São Paulo School of Economics at the Getulio Vargas Foundation—FGV. He is the coordinator for Economic Modeling at the Center of Global Trade at FGV. His research areas include: international trade theory, Computerized General Equilibrium Models, global value chains and costs estimates for infrastructure and non-tariff barriers.

Daniel S. Hamilton is the Austrian Marshall Plan Foundation Professor and Director of the Center for Transatlantic Relations at the Paul H. Nitze School of Advanced International Studies, Johns Hopkins University. He also serves as Executive Director of the American Consortium on EU Studies, designated by the European Commission as the EU Center of Excellence Washington, DC. He has been a consultant for Microsoft and an advisor to the U.S. Business Roundtable, the Transatlantic Business Dialogue, and the European-American Business Council. Recent books include *The Transatlantic Economy 2014*; *Atlantic Rising: Changing Commercial Dynamics in the Atlantic Basin*; *Open Ukraine: Changing Course towards a European Future*; *Europe's Economic Crisis*; *Transatlantic 2020: A Tale of Four Futures*, and *Europe 2020: Competitive or Complacent?* He has served in a variety of senior positions in the U.S. State Department, including as Deputy Assistant Secretary of State.

Eveline Herfkens is a Visiting Scholar at the Paul H. Nitze School of Advanced International Studies and a Senior Fellow at the Center for Transatlantic Relations. She was the Founder and Executive Coordinator for the United Nations Millennium Development Goals Campaign, appointed by UN Secretary General Kofi Annan in 2002, and has served as Minister for Development Cooperation of the Netherlands; Ambassador and Permanent Representative of the Netherlands, United Organizations and the WTO in Geneva; member of the Board of Executive Directors of the World Bank Group; and a Member of Parliament in the Netherlands.

Kemal Kirişci is the TÜSIAD senior fellow and director of the Center on the United States and Europe's Turkey Project at the Brookings Institution, with an expertise in Turkish foreign policy and migration studies. Before joining Brookings, he was a professor of international relations and held the Jean Monnet chair in European integration in the department of political science and international relations at Boğaziçi University in Istanbul. His areas of research interest include EU-Turkish relations, U.S.-Turkish relations, Turkish foreign and trade policies, European integration, immigration issues, ethnic conflicts and refugee movements. Recent publications include *Syrian Refugees and Turkey's Challenges: Going Beyond Hospitality* (Brookings, May 2014) and *Turkey and the Transatlantic Trade and Investment Partnership: Boosting the Model Partnership with the United States* (Brookings, September 2013). He is the author of several books, including *Turkey and Its Neighbors: Foreign Relations in Transition* (co-authored with R. Linden et al; Lynne Rienner, 2011); *Turkey In World Politics: An Emerging Multi-Regional Power* (Co-edited with B. Rubin; Lynne Rienner, 2001); and *The Kurdish Question and Turkey: An Example of a Trans-State Ethnic Conflict* (co-authored with G. Winrow, Frank Cass,1997).

Charles A. Kupchan is Professor of International Affairs in the School of Foreign Service and Government Department at Georgetown University, and Whitney H. Shepardson Senior Fellow at the Council on Foreign Relations. During 2013–2014, he was also a Senior Fellow at the Transatlantic Academy. He was Director for European Affairs on the National Security Council during the first Clinton administration. He is the author of *No One's World: The West, the Rising Rest, and the Coming Global Turn* (2012), *How Enemies Become Friends: The Sources of Stable Peace* (2010), and other books and articles on international affairs. He was educated at Harvard University and Oxford University.

Edward Lucas is a senior editor at the *Economist*. He is the author of several books, including *The New Cold War* (Bloomsbury), first published in 2008, which gave warning of the dangers posed by the Putin regime in Moscow. It has just been republished in an updated and revised edition.

Tamás Novák is an Austrian Marshall Plan Foundation Fellow at the Center for Transatlantic Relations, Paul H. Nitze School of Advanced International Studies (SAIS), Johns Hopkins University; Deputy Director of the Institute of World Economics, Hungarian Academy of Sciences; and Associate Professor at the Budapest Business School. He has been a senior analyst at the Hungarian Development Bank and adviser in the Ministry of Foreign Affairs. He has worked on the economic problems of Central European countries and the economics of regional integrations. He has published widely on global economic issues with special emphasis on transition economies and economic convergence. He serves on the editorial board of *Development and Finance*, a bilingual Hungarian economic quarterly. He has a Ph.D. in International Relations and an MA in Economics from the Budapest University of Economics.

Michael G. Plummer is the Eni Professor of International Economics at the Johns Hopkins University, SAIS, and Director of SAIS Europe. He is also Editor-in-Chief of the *Journal of Asian Economics*; President, American Committee for Asian Economic Studies (ACAES); and (non-resident) Senior Fellow at the East-West Center. He also served as Head of the Development Division of the OECD (2010–2012). Previous to these positions he was Associate Professor of Economics at Brandeis University (1992–2001), where he received tenure in 1998. He has also been a Fulbright Chair in Economics and Pew Fellow in International Affairs, Harvard University; and a research professor at Kobe University. He has worked on numerous projects for international organizations, development and other government agencies, and regional development banks. His Ph.D. in economics is from Michigan State University.

Charles Ries is Vice President, International at the RAND Corporation, where he oversees RAND's international offices, and a Senior Fellow whose research has focused on the economics of development. While on a leave of absence from RAND in 2010, Ries was executive vice president of the Clinton Bush Haiti Fund. His three decades in the U.S. diplomatic service included an assignment as Coordinator for Economic Transition in Iraq at the U.S. Embassy in Baghdad (2007–2008), where he was responsible for oversight and coordination of assistance and economic policy initiatives. Before that, he was U.S. Ambassador to Greece (2004–2007), and Principal Deputy Assistant

Secretary of State for European Affairs (2000–2004). In earlier assignments, Ries was the Minister Counselor for Economic Affairs at the U.S. Embassy in London, and Minister Counselor for Economic Affairs at the U.S. Mission to the European Union. He served as Deputy Assistant U.S. Trade Representative for North American Affairs and was a member of the NAFTA negotiating team.

Colin Robertson, a former Canadian diplomat, is Senior Strategic Advisor for McKenna, Long and Aldridge LLP and working with the Canadian Council of Chief Executives. He is Vice President and Fellow at the Canadian Defence and Foreign Affairs Institute and Executive Fellow at the University of Calgary's School of Public Policy. He is a Distinguished Senior Fellow at the Norman Paterson School of International Affairs at Carleton University. He is chair of the board of Canada World Youth. He is a member of the board of the Conference of Defence Associations Institute and the advisory board of the North American Research Partnership. He is a past president of the National Capital Branch of the Canadian International Council. He is an Honorary Captain (Royal Canadian Navy) assigned to the Strategic Communications Directorate. He is s regular contributor on foreign affairs to the *Globe and Mail* and other publications.

Thomas Straubhaar is the director of the Hamburg Institute of International Economics (HWWI) and University Professor of Economics, especially International Economic Relations at the University of Hamburg. He is also a nonresident fellow with the Transatlantic Academy. He has published widely about causes and consequences of globalization, especially the economics of international labor migration and the future of the European economy.

Vera Thorstensen is a professor at the São Paulo School of Economics at the Getulio Vargas Foundation—FGV. She is also the Head of the Center on Global Trade and Investment at FGV and Head of the WTO Chair in Brazil. She was the economic advisor of the Mission of Brazil to the WTO from 1995 until 2010 and Chair of the Committee on Rules of Origin for seven years. Her research areas include: trade regulation, preferential trade, trade and exchange rate, new barriers to trade (TBT-SPS), value chains and WTO.